NNAT

Naglieri Nonverbal Ability Test®

REASONING
BY
ANALOGY

A step by step STUDY GUIDE

GRADE 3

by MindMine

# Why this book?

Cognitive abilities are brain-based skills related with the mechanisms of learning, memorizing, and paying attention rather than actual knowledge that was learned. **The more you practice, the more you develop** your cognitive flexibility.

- This book is designed to teach concepts and skills in a way kids understand with ease.

- Concepts are taught step by step and introduced incrementally.

- The focus of this book is to provide a solid foundation to fundamental skills. All the skills taught in the book will collectively increase the knowledge and will help kids to prepare and take the test confidently.

- Practice tests that are available in the market may not provide all the concepts needed. This book is aimed to give both concepts and practice.

Who should buy this book?

- 3rd graders taking NNAT test (NNAT2)

- 2nd graders planning to take NNAT (Any Form)

- 1st, 2nd and 3rd graders seeking to enrich their Nonverbal reasoning and Problem-solving skills

📚 What is covered?

This book extensively covers **REASONING BY ANALOGY** section of **NNAT Test** with 300 unique questions and 400 secondary questions.

📚 **2 FULL LENGTH PRACTICE TESTS with Answers**

Full Length Practice Test#1	15 Questions
Full Length Practice Test#2	15 Questions

📚 **FUNDAMENTAL CONCEPTS**

📚 **BASIC PROBLEMS**   100 Questions

📚 **NNAT QUESTIONS**   200 Questions

📚 Table of Contents

ANSWERS

Concept	Page#

Reasoning by Analogy

Find the figure that should go in the box with Question Mark

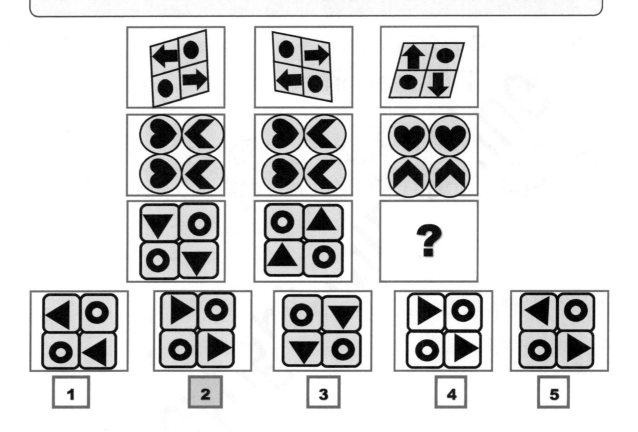

ANSWER: 2

Reasoning by Analogy - HOW TO SOLVE?

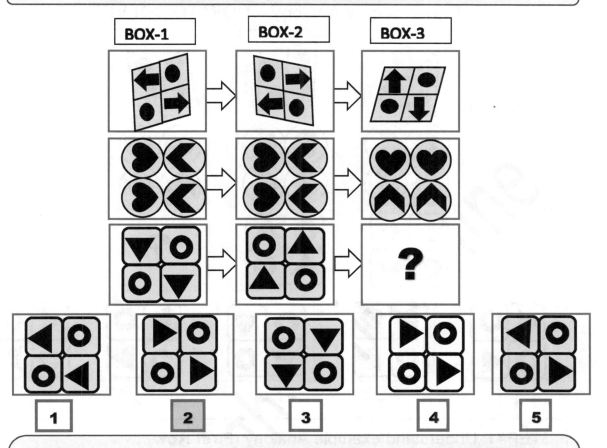

| BOX-1 | BOX-2 | BOX-3 |

1   2   3   4   5

STEP#1: Understand example Analogy (**First Row**). Read the way arrows are pointed. If no arrows, read LEFT to RIGHT)

STEP#2: **Further** understand example Analogy (**Second Row**). Read LEFT to RIGHT.

STEP#3: Apply same Analogy to question. Read LEFT to RIGHT.

**DO NOT Copy Example characteristics (such as Shape, Color, Pattern, Size, Position, Sides, Angle etc.,)

Reasoning by Analogy – HOW TO SOLVE?

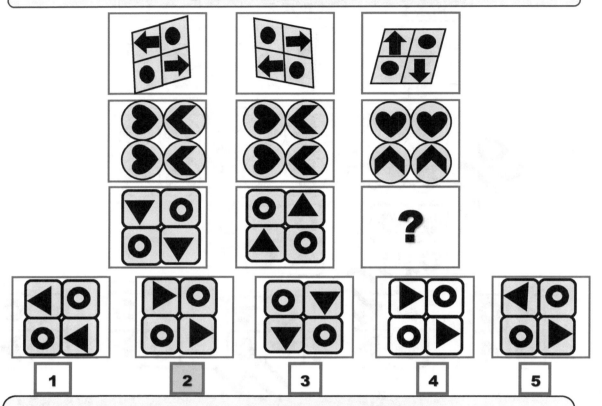

STEP#1: Understand example Analogy (**First Row**).

FLIP Sideways. Then TURN

STEP#2: **Further** understand example Analogy (**Second Row**). **FLIP Sideways. Then TURN CLOCKWISE**

STEP#3: Apply same Analogy to question. Read LEFT to RIGHT.
ANSWER: 2

1 is WRONG -Turned Counter Clockwise

3 is WRONG -FLIPPED upside Down

4 is WRONG - Background Color is not Gray

5 is WRONG -Only one Triangle is Turned Clockwise

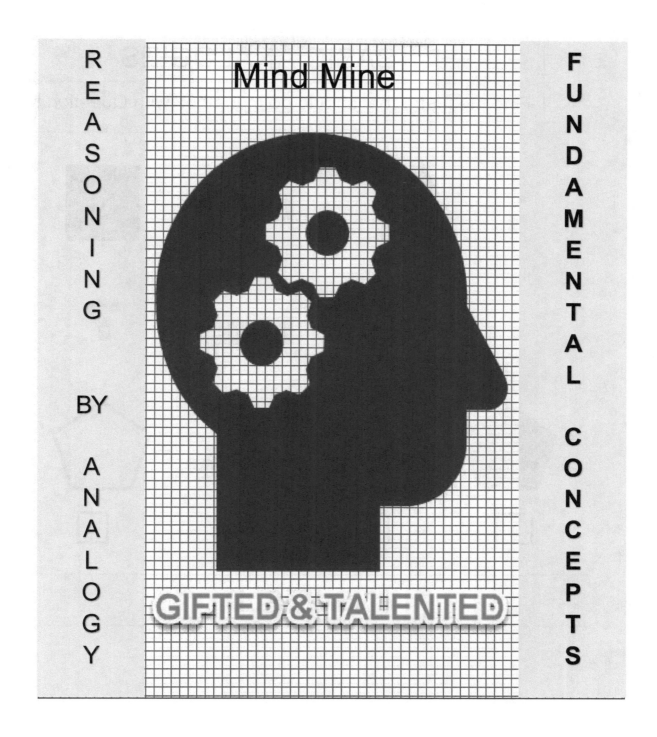

Mind Mine

REASONING BY ANALOGY

FUNDAMENTAL CONCEPTS

GIFTED & TALENTED

4

BASIC ANALOGIES

Find the figure that should go in the box with Question Mark

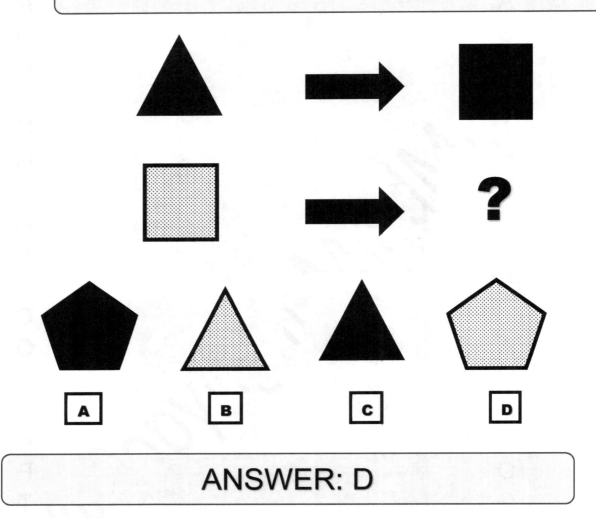

A

B

C

D

ANSWER: D

5

BASIC ANALOGIES

HOW TO SOLVE?

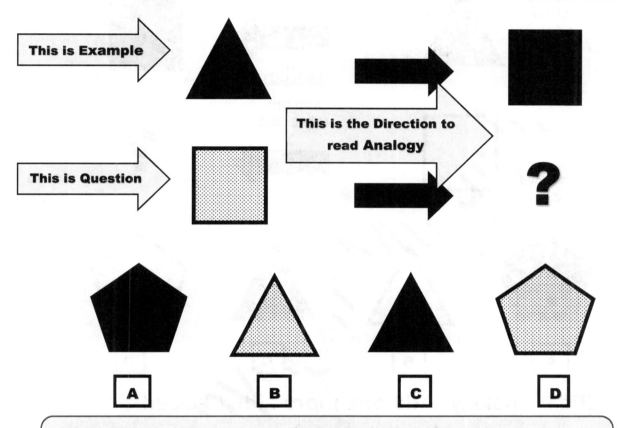

This is Example

This is Question

This is the Direction to read Analogy

?

A   B   C   D

STEP#1: Understand example Analogy. Read the way arrow is pointed (LEFT to RIGHT)

STEP#2: Apply same Analogy to question. Read the way arrow is pointed (LEFT to RIGHT).

**DO NOT Copy Example characteristics (such as Shape, Color, Pattern, Size, Position, Sides, Angle etc.,)

BASIC ANALOGIES

HOW TO SOLVE?

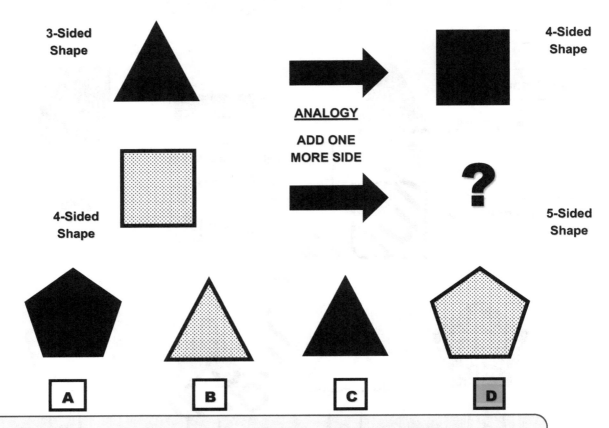

3-Sided Shape

ANALOGY

ADD ONE MORE SIDE

4-Sided Shape

4-Sided Shape

?

5-Sided Shape

A   B   C   D

STEP#1: Analogy: **Add one more side** (3-sided shape becomes a 4-sided shape)

STEP#2: Apply Analogy: **4-sided shape becomes a 5-sided shape**, when one more side is added. **Answer Choices B & C are WRONG**

DO NOT Copy Example characteristics (such as Shape (Square), Color (Black). **Answer Choice A is WRONG.

** Read the way Arrow is pointed (Left to Right). **Answer Choice C is WRONG.**

FUNDAMENTAL
CONCEPTS

Figures with NO (Zero) Sides

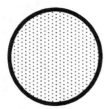  

Figures with ONE Side

Figures with TWO Sides

   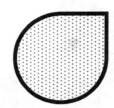

FUNDAMENTAL CONCEPTS

Figures with THREE Sides

3-sides of
Equal Length

2-sides of
Equal Length

NO-sides of
Equal Length

Figures with THREE Sides

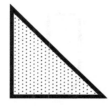

RIGHT Angle
Triangle

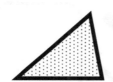

ACUTE Angle
Triangle

OBTUSE Angle
Triangle

Figures with FOUR Sides

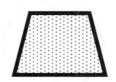

Figures with FOUR Sides

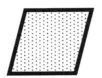 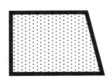 

Figures with FIVE Sides

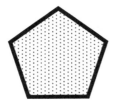  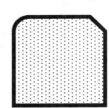 

Figures with SIX Sides

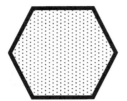  

Figures with SEVEN Sides

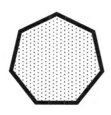 

Figures with EIGHT Sides

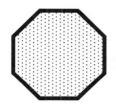 

Figures with NINE Sides

12

Figures with TEN Sides

Figures with TWELVE Sides

FUNDAMENTAL CONCEPTS

POSITION

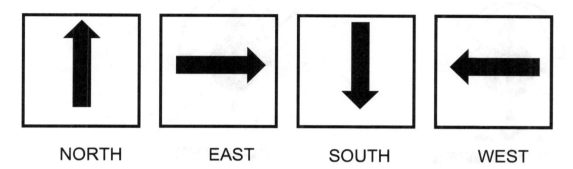

NORTH EAST SOUTH WEST

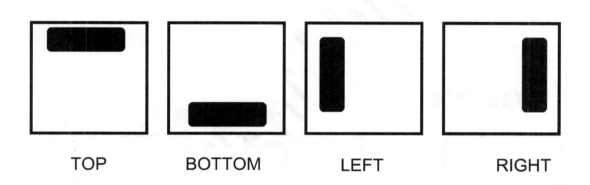

TOP BOTTOM LEFT RIGHT

CORNER#1 CORNER#2 CORNER#3 CORNER#4

14

FUNDAMENTAL CONCEPTS

Rotation

CLOCK-WISE

COUNTER CLOCK-WISE

COLOR

FILL

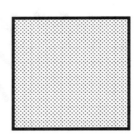

PATTERN

OUTLINE

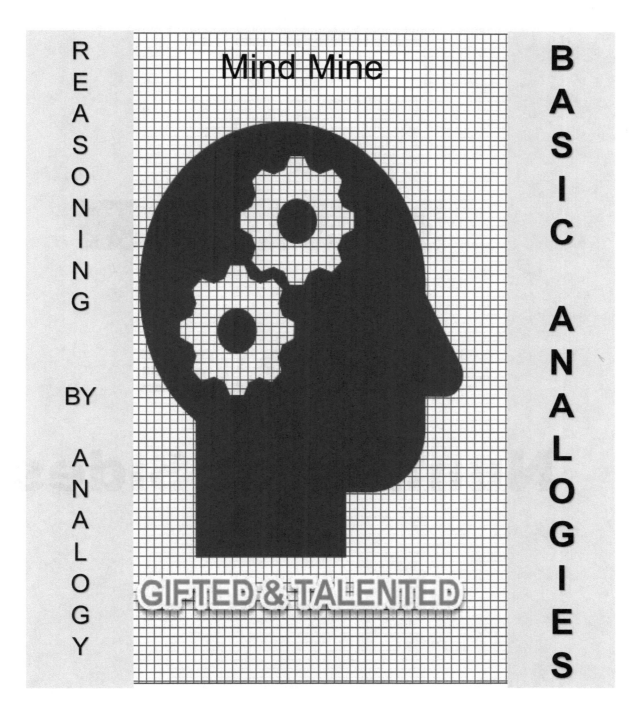

Mind Mine

REASONING BY ANALOGY

BASIC ANALOGIES

16

ANALOGY

CHANGE

Number of Sides

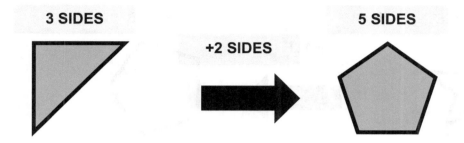

ADD ONE or MORE SIDES

3 SIDES   +2 SIDES   5 SIDES

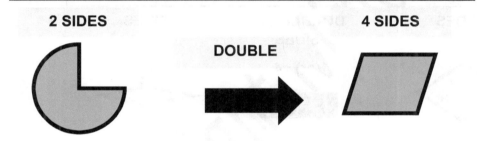

DOUBLE the NUMBER OF SIDES

2 SIDES   DOUBLE   4 SIDES

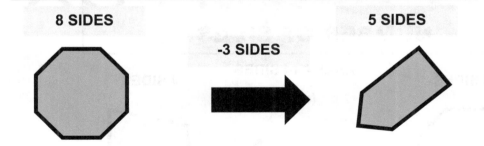

SUBTRACT ONE or MORE SIDES

8 SIDES   -3 SIDES   5 SIDES

18

HALF the NUMBER OF SIDES

10 SIDES **5 SIDES**

HALF

ADD or DOUBLE
NUMBER OF SIDES

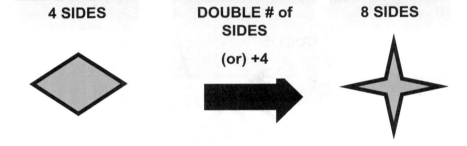

4 SIDES DOUBLE # of SIDES **8 SIDES**

(or) +4

SUBTRACT or HALF
NUMBER OF SIDES

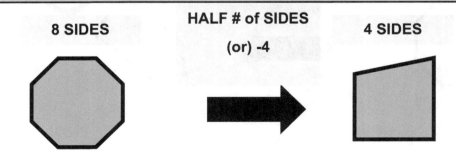

HALF # of SIDES

(or) -4

8 SIDES **4 SIDES**

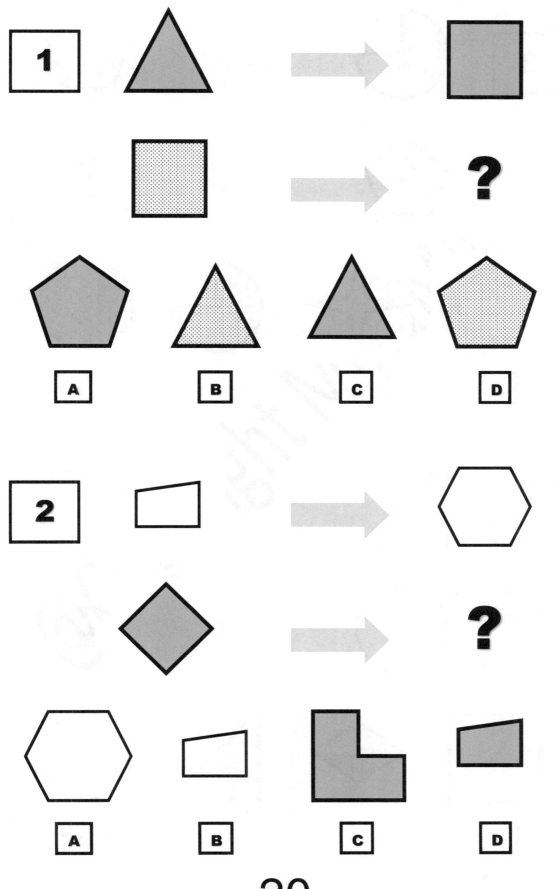

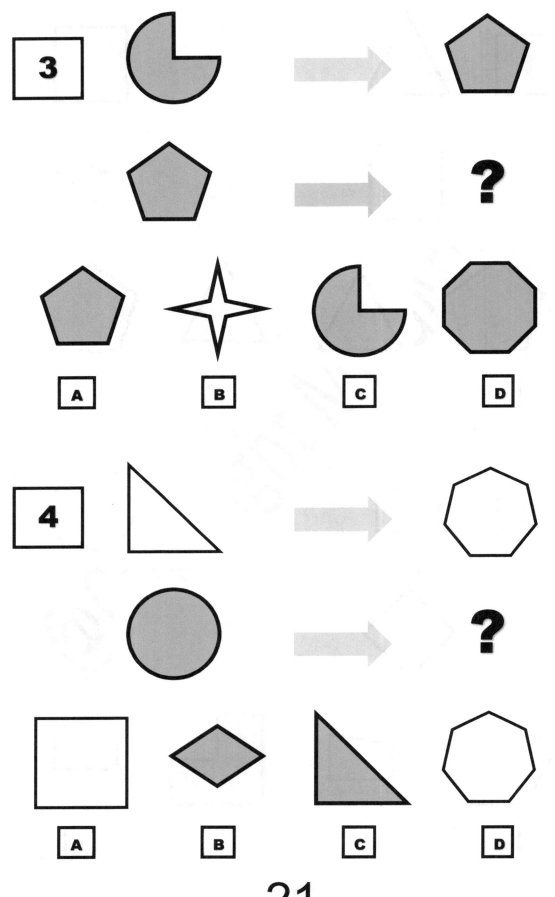

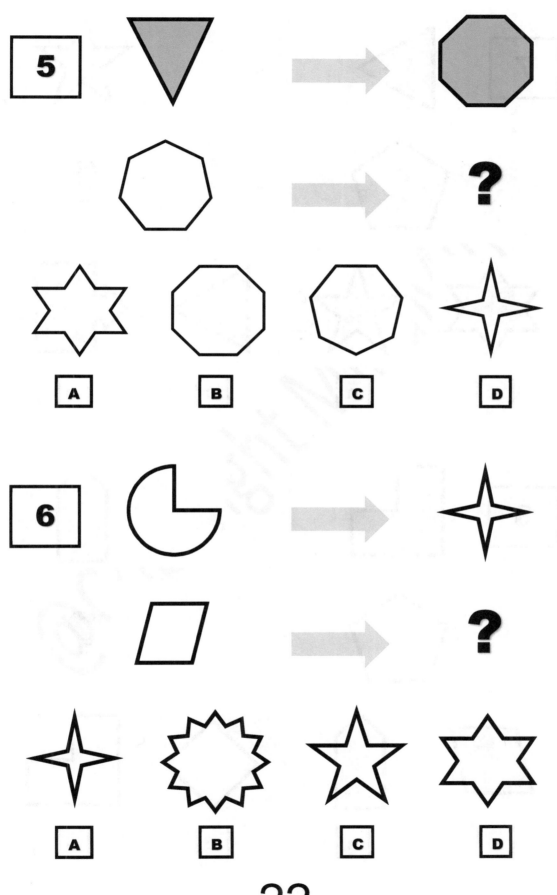

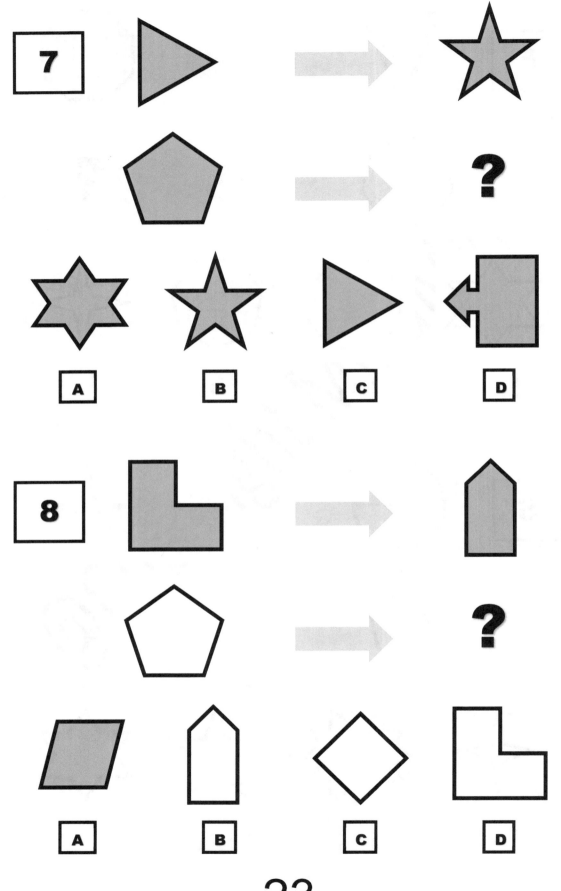

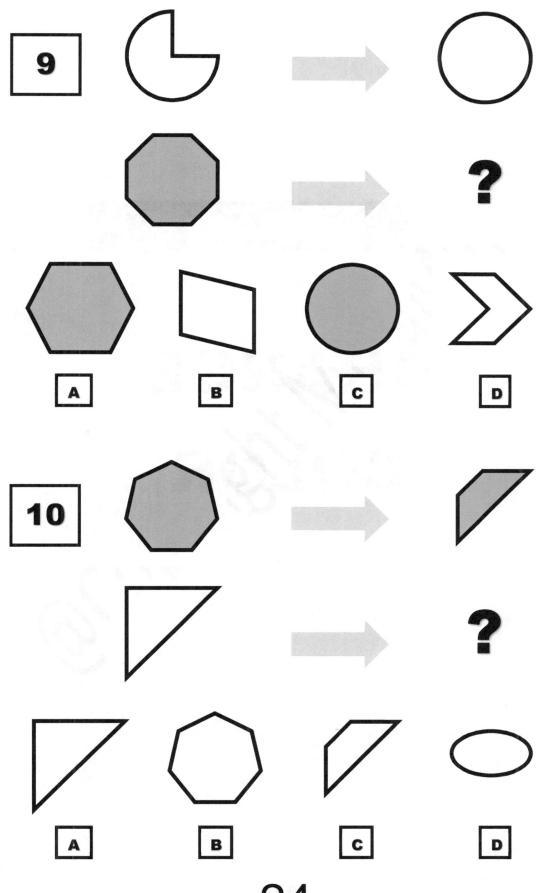

ANALOGY

CHANGE

COLOR

Change Color

Change Color

To BLACK

Change Pattern

Change Pattern

To
Horizontal Lines

Change OUTLINE

Change Outline

To
Dotted Lines

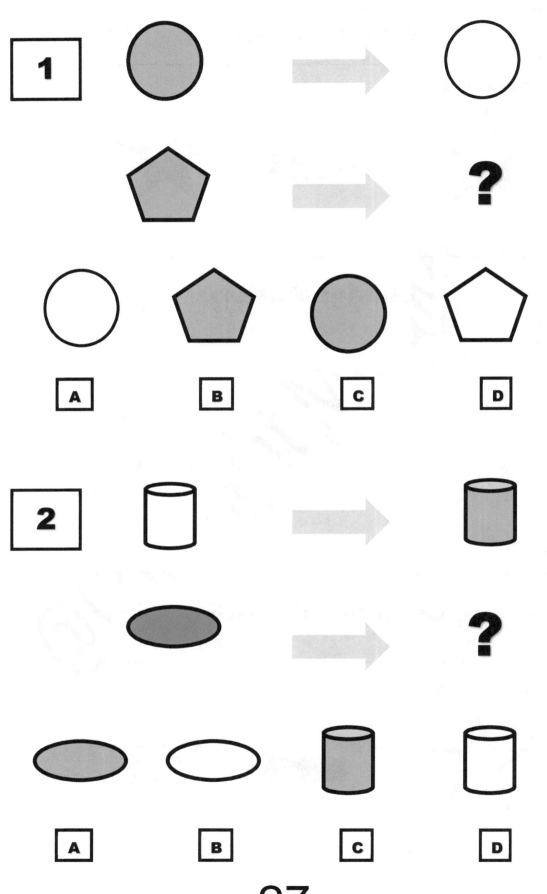

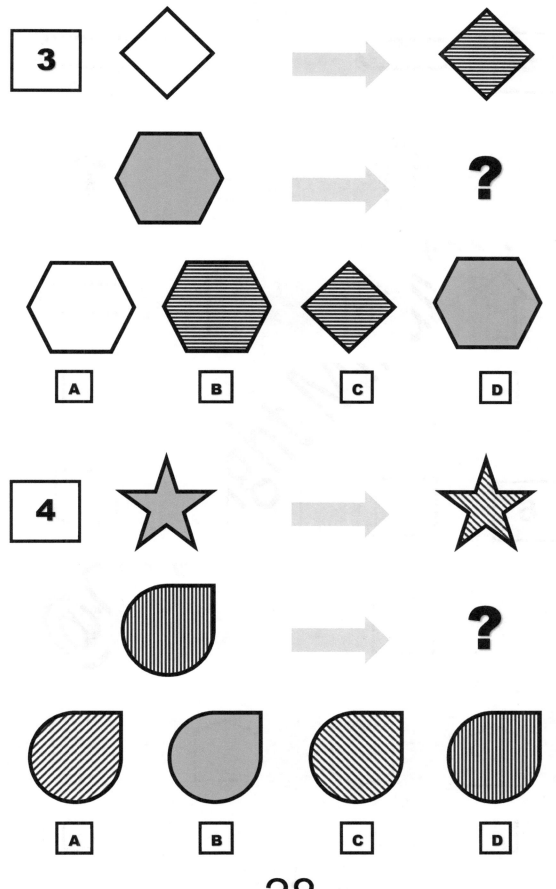

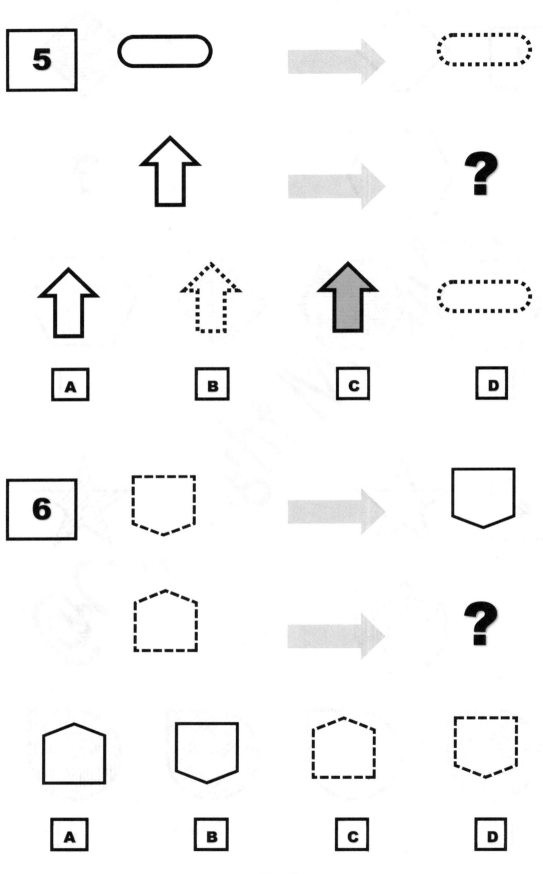

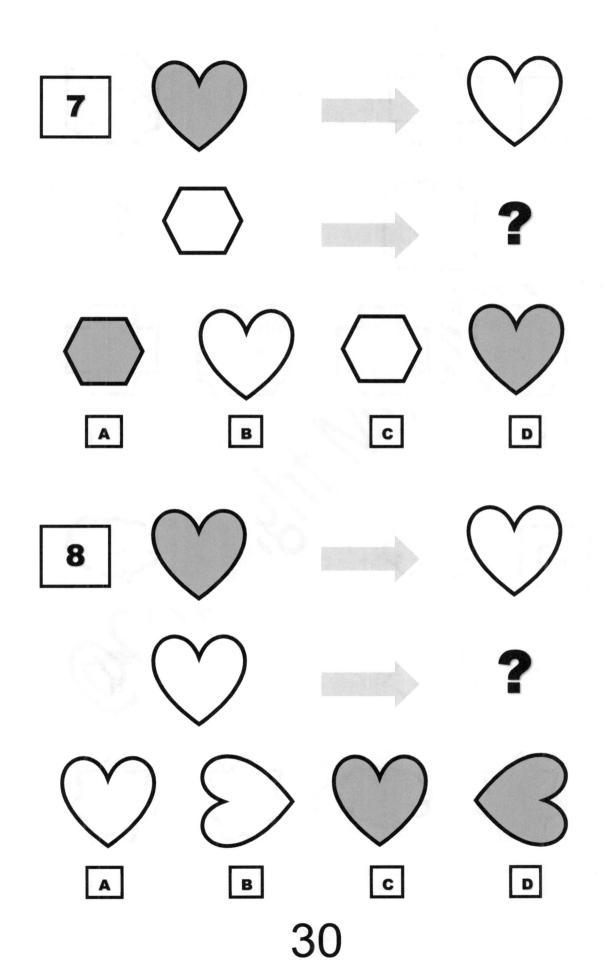

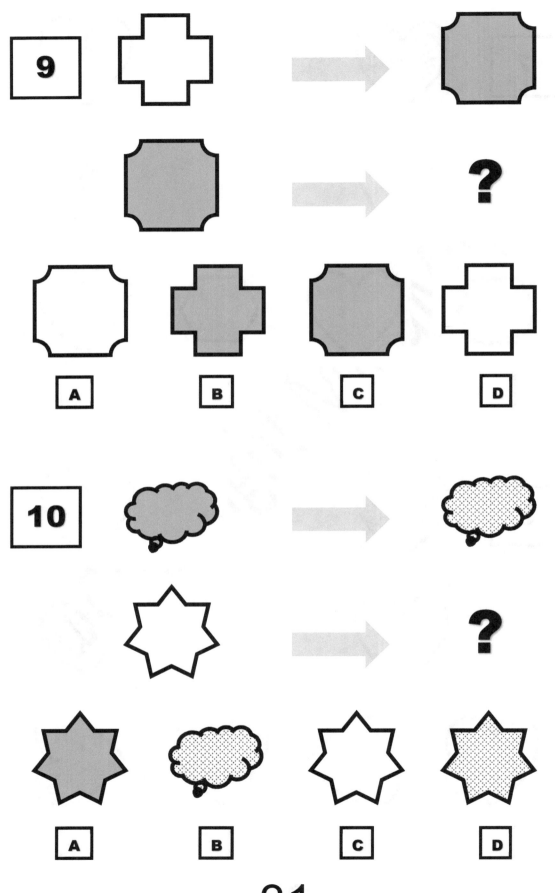

ANALOGY

CHANGE

Size

Change Size - Make BIG
(Increase LENGTH & WIDTH)

Make Big

Change Size – Make SMALL
(Decrease LENGTH & WIDTH)

Make Small

Change Size
Increase Length (or Base) ONLY

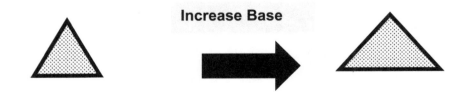

Increase Base

Change Size
Increase HEIGHT ONLY

Increase Height

Change Size
Decrease Length (or Base) ONLY

Decrease Length

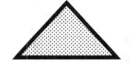 

Change Size
Decrease HEIGHT ONLY

Decrease Height

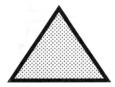  

34

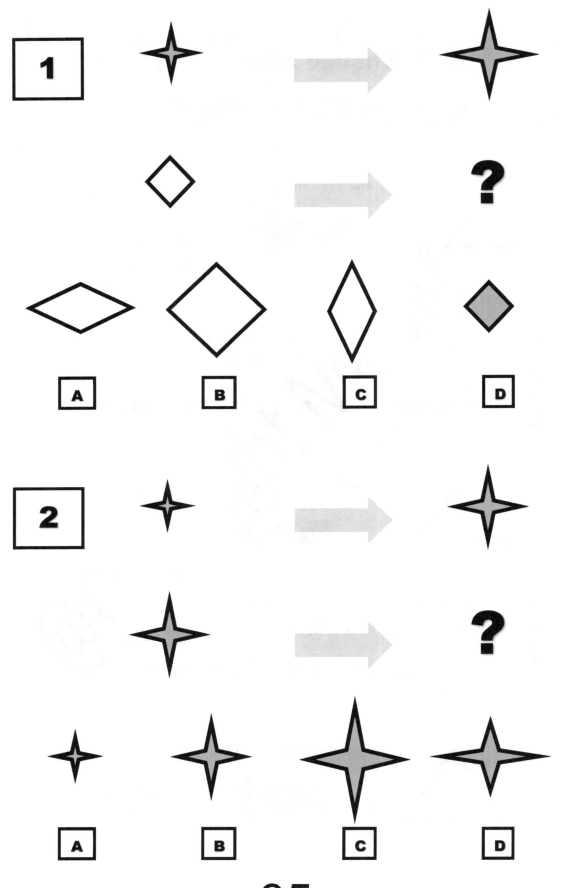

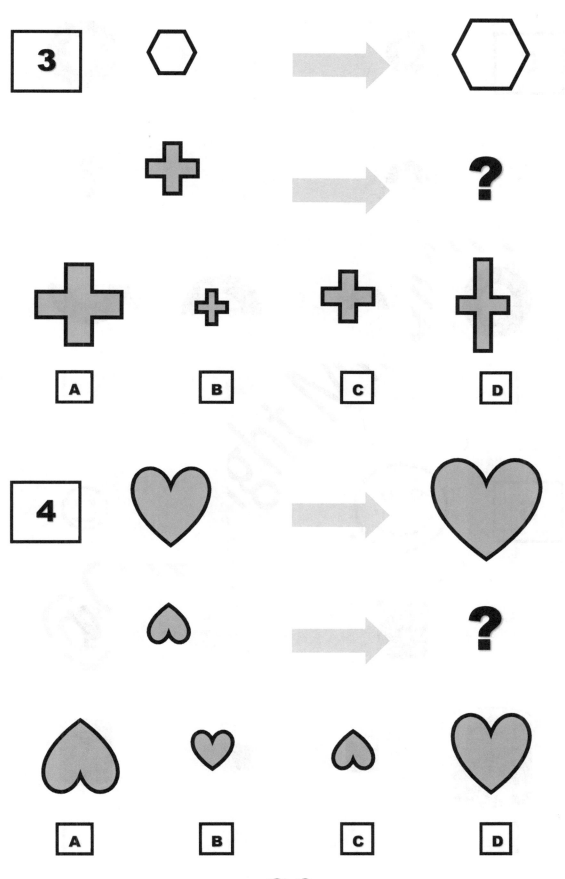

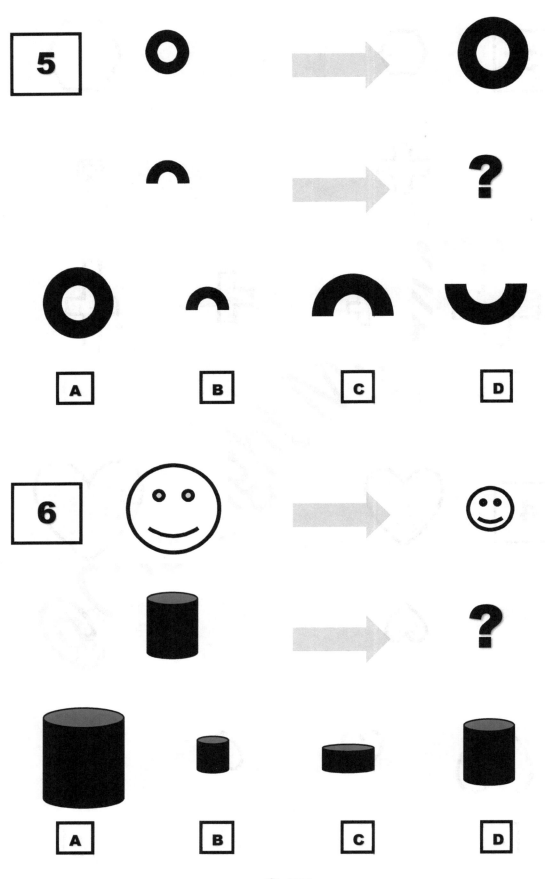

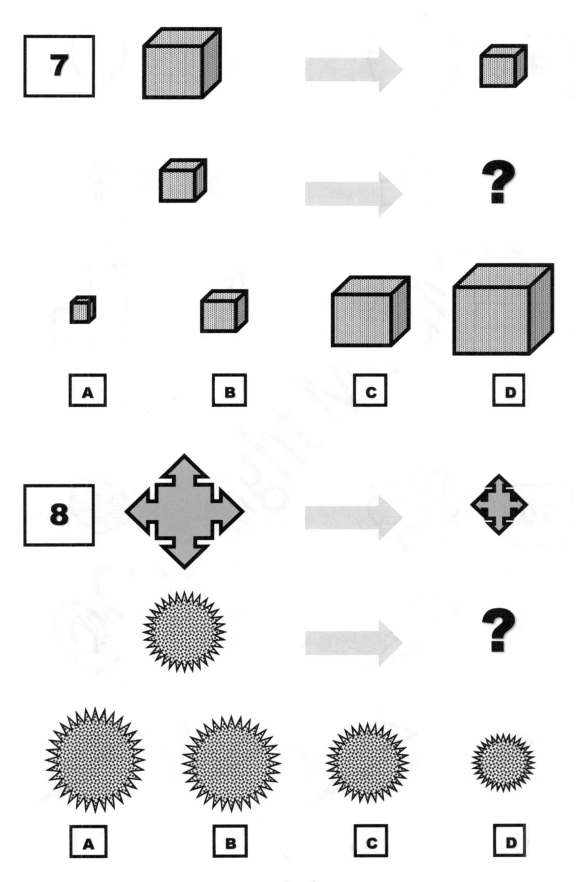

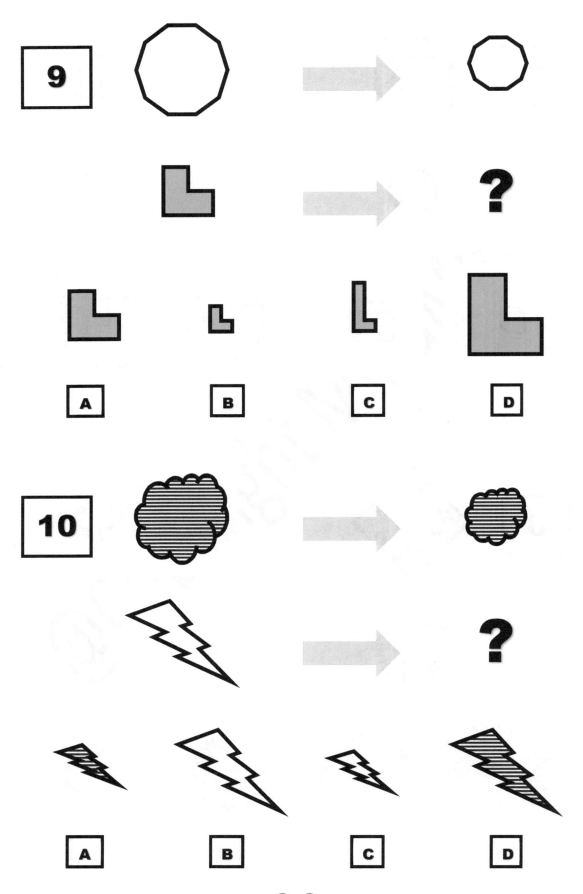

39

FLIP
(REFLECTION)

FLIP UPSIDE DOWN

FLIP

UPSIDE DOWN

FLIP SIDEWAYS

FLIP

SIDEWAYS

FLIP UPSIDE DOWN

FLIP

UPSIDE DOWN

Note: Same shape results when flipped upside down

FLIP SIDEWAYS

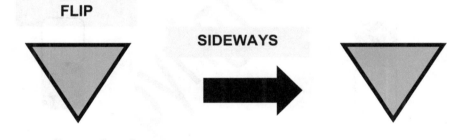

FLIP

SIDEWAYS

Note: Same shape results when flipped sideways

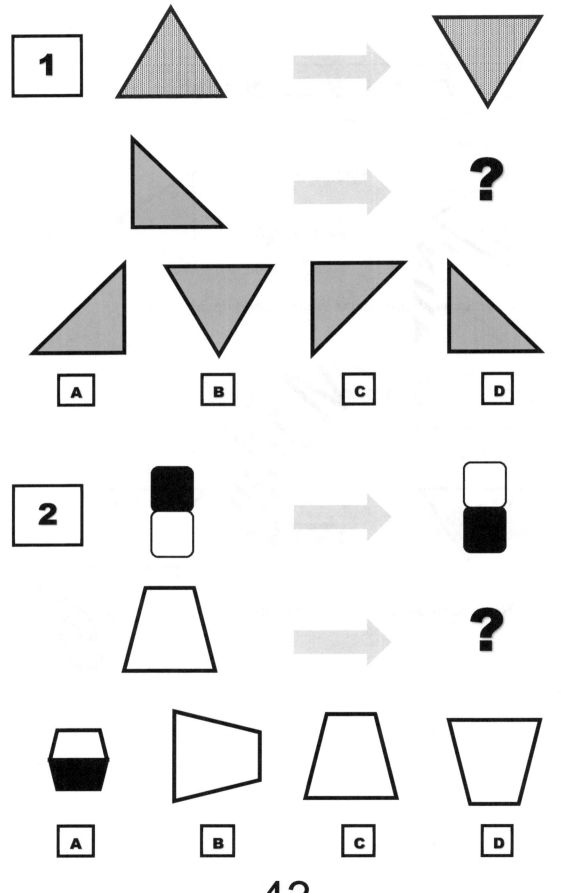

43

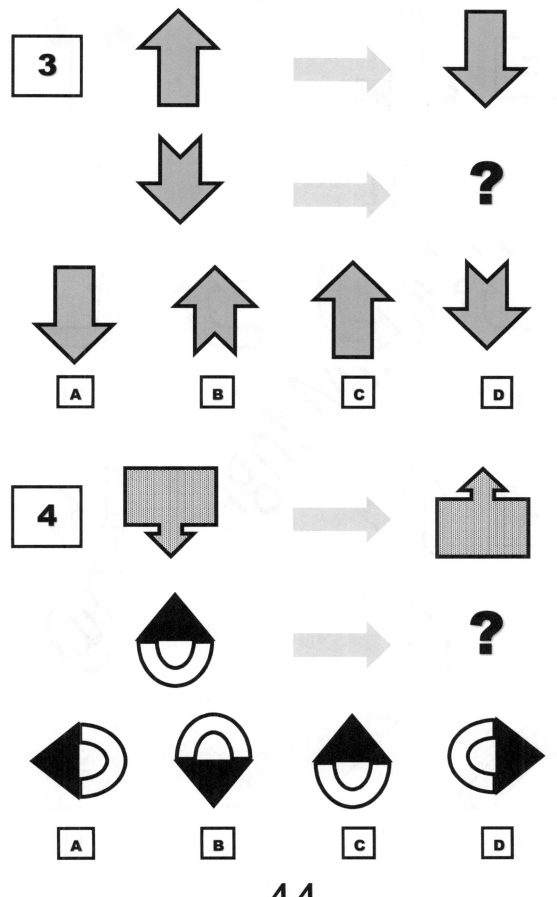

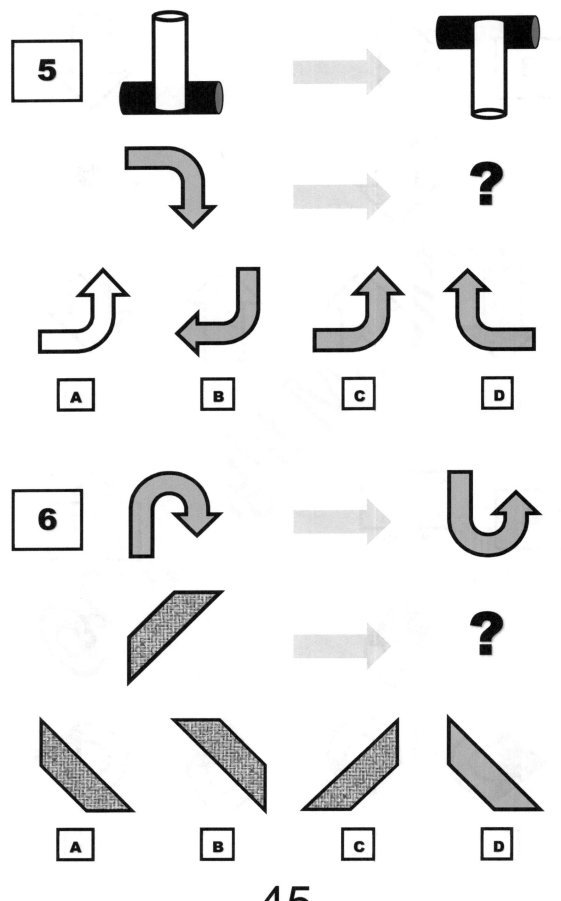

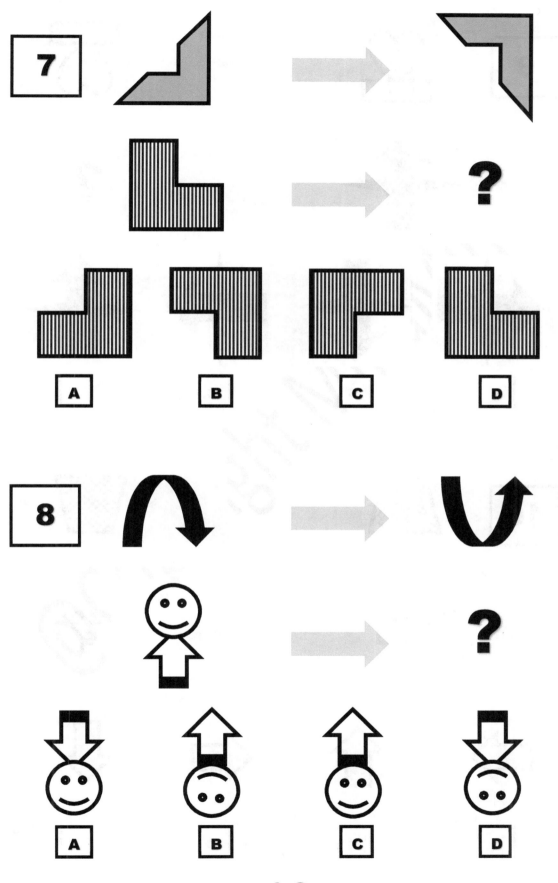

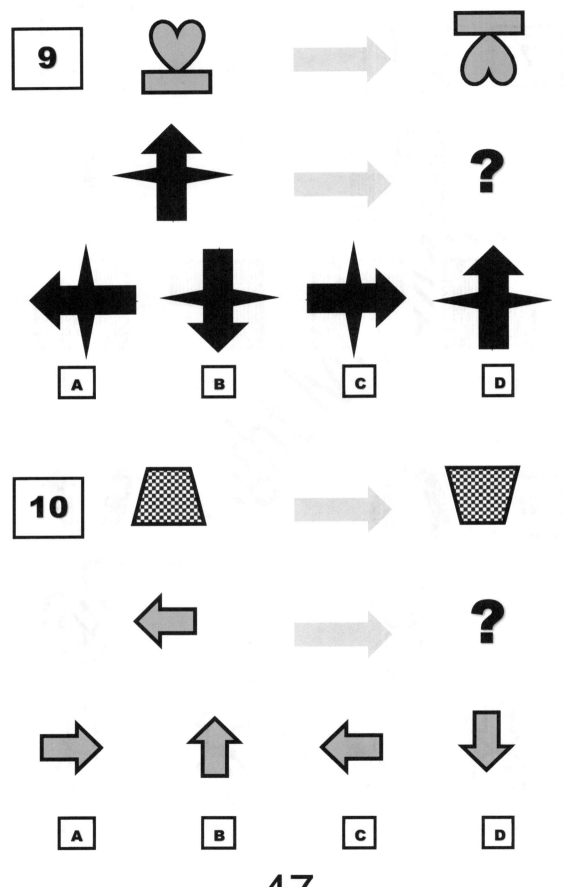

CUT FIGURE

CUT TOP

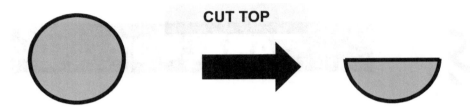

CUT BOTTOM

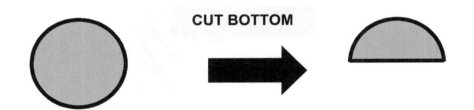

49

CUT LEFT

CUT LEFT

CUT RIGHT

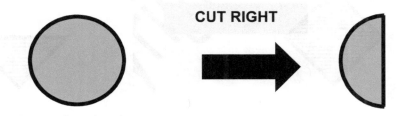

CUT RIGHT

50

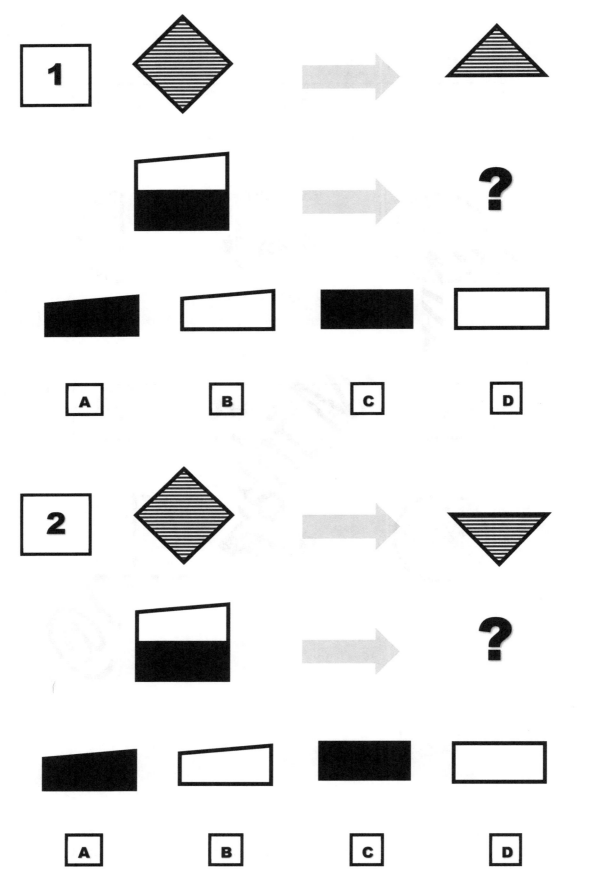

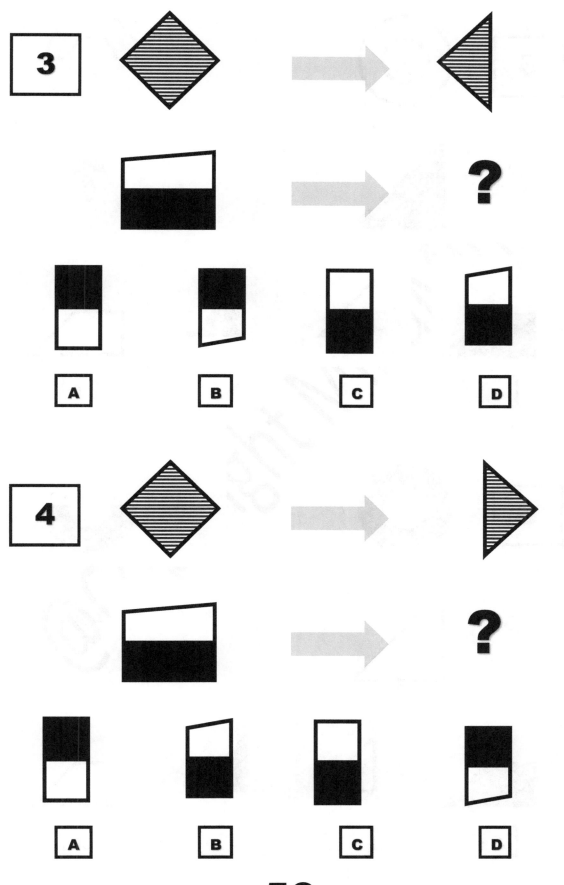

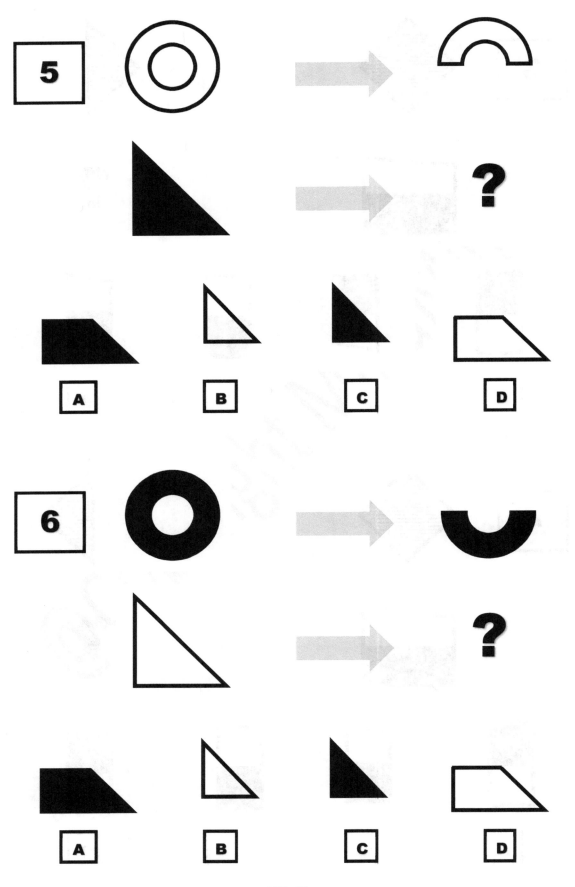

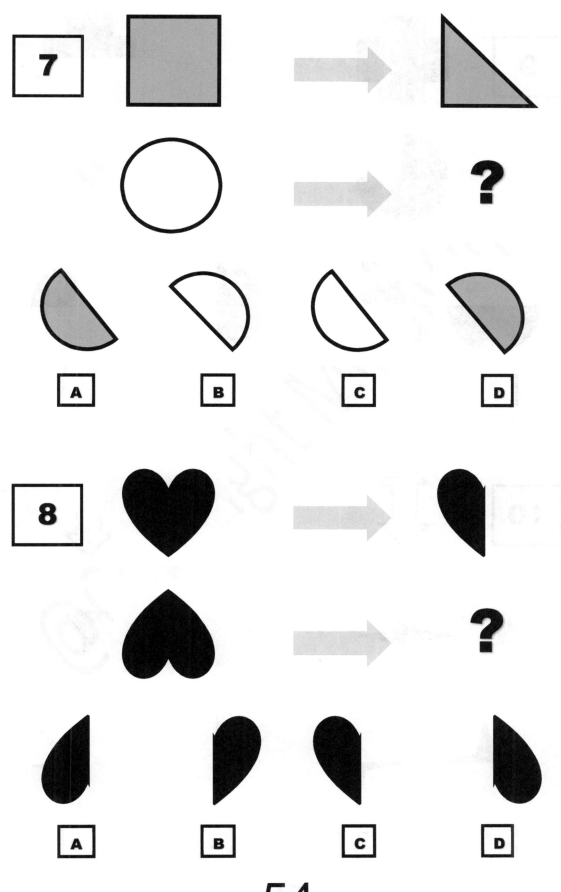

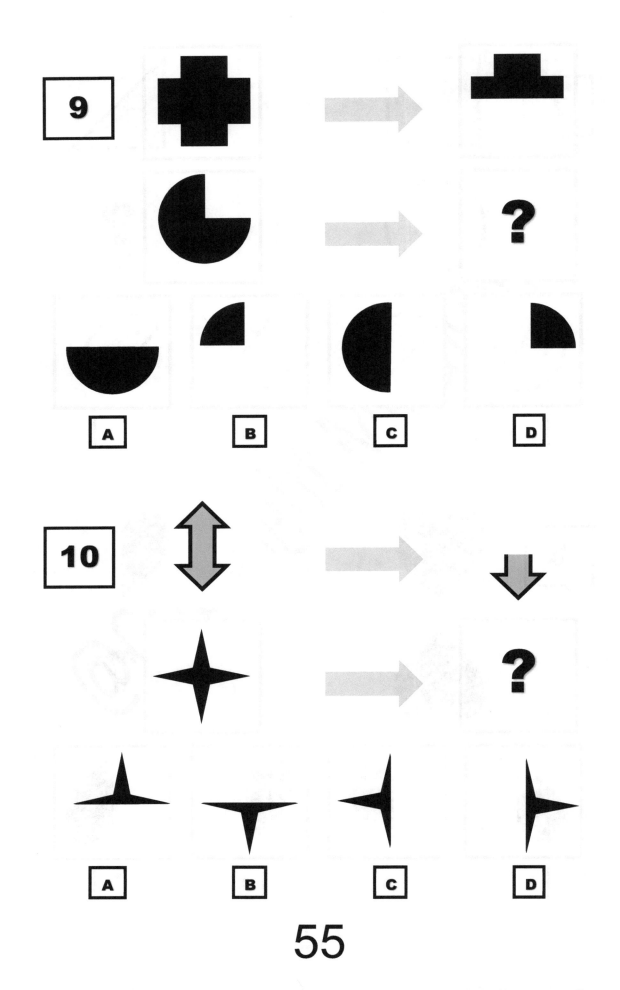

ANALOGY

ADD (or)
REMOVE
A Figure

ADD a FIGURE

Add a Figure

Inside

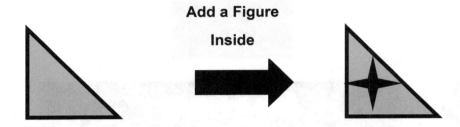

ADD SAME FIGURE

Add SAME Figure

Inside

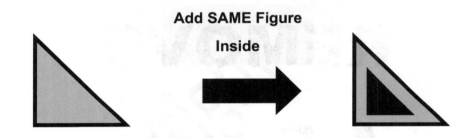

ADD a FIGURE

Add a Figure

OUTSIDE

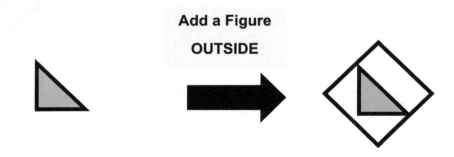

REMOVE a FIGURE

Remove a
Figure

REMOVE a Side

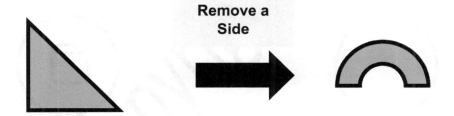

Remove a
Side

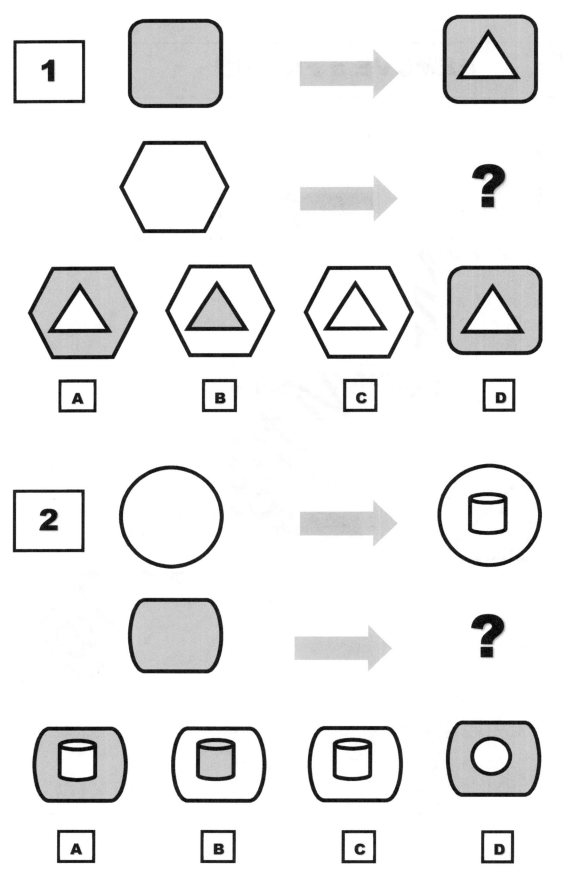

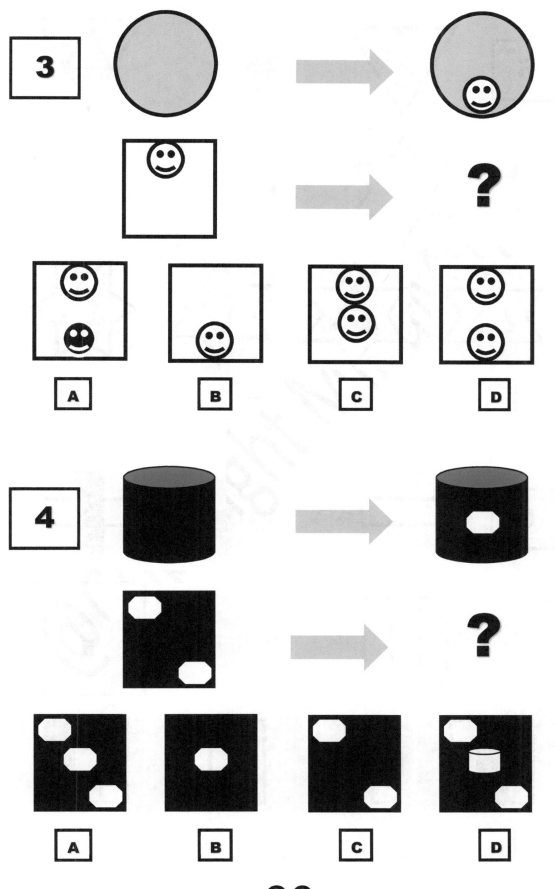

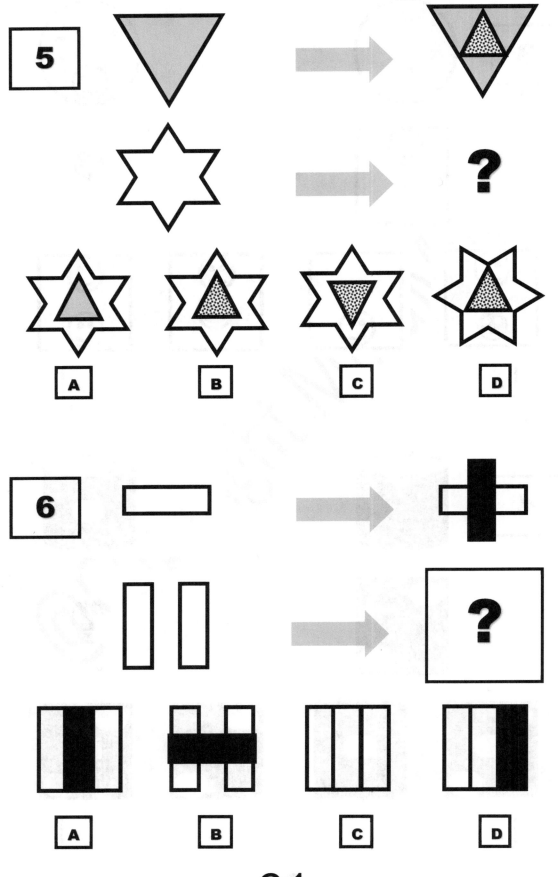

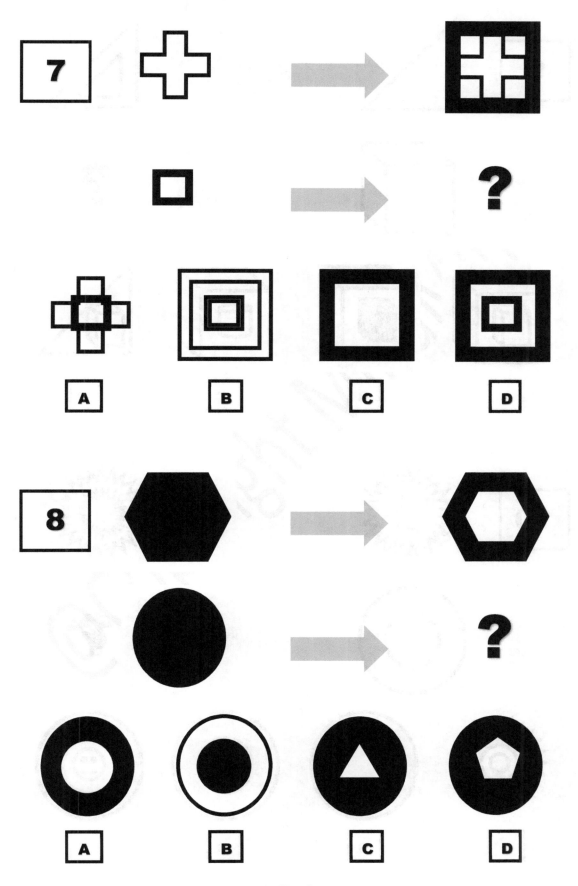

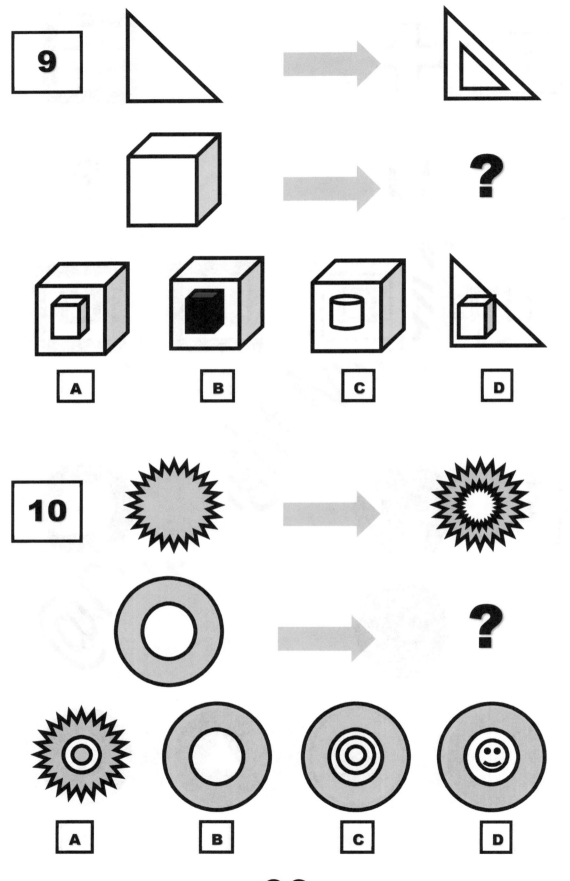

ANALOGY

MOVE

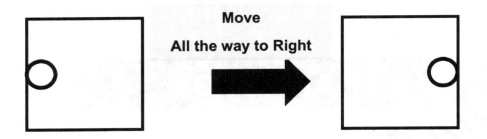

65

MOVE FIGURE

ALL THE WAY TO DOWN

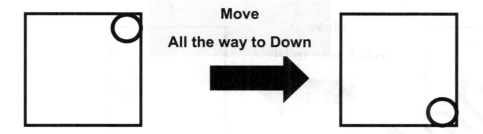

Move
All the way to Down

MOVE FIGURE

HALF WAY TO LEFT

Move
HALF way to Left

MOVE FIGURE

HALF WAY TO RIGHT

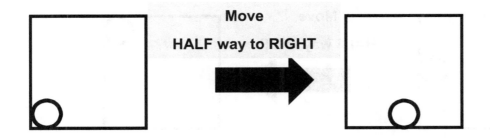

Move
HALF way to RIGHT

MOVE FIGURE
HALF WAY TO UP

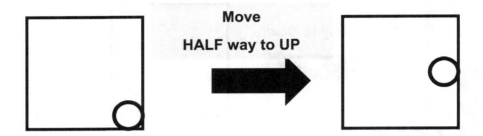

Move
HALF way to UP

MOVE FIGURE
HALF WAY TO DOWN

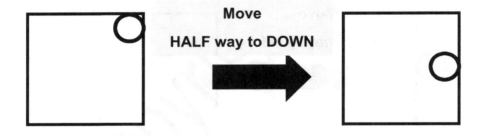

Move
HALF way to DOWN

MOVE FIGURE
HALF WAY TO UP

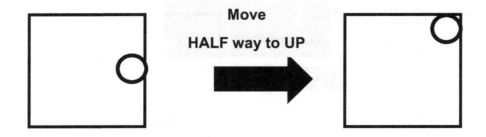

Move
HALF way to UP

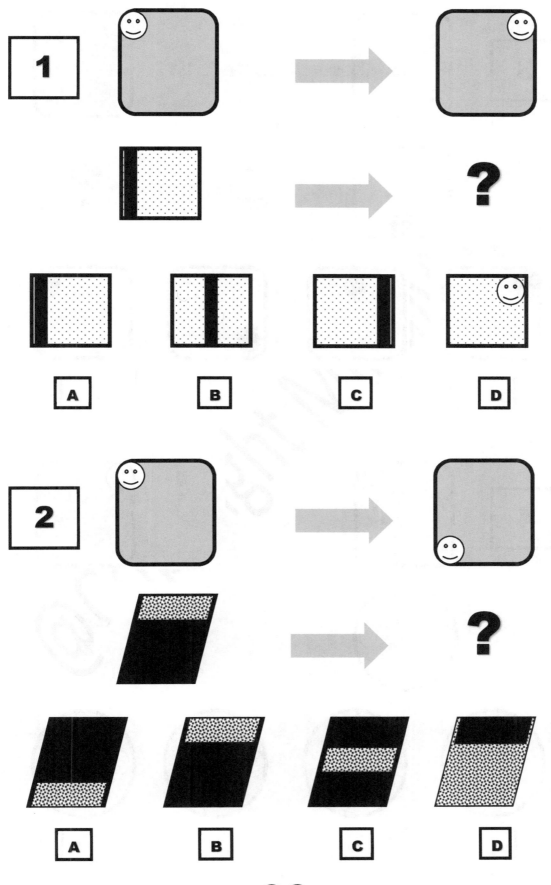

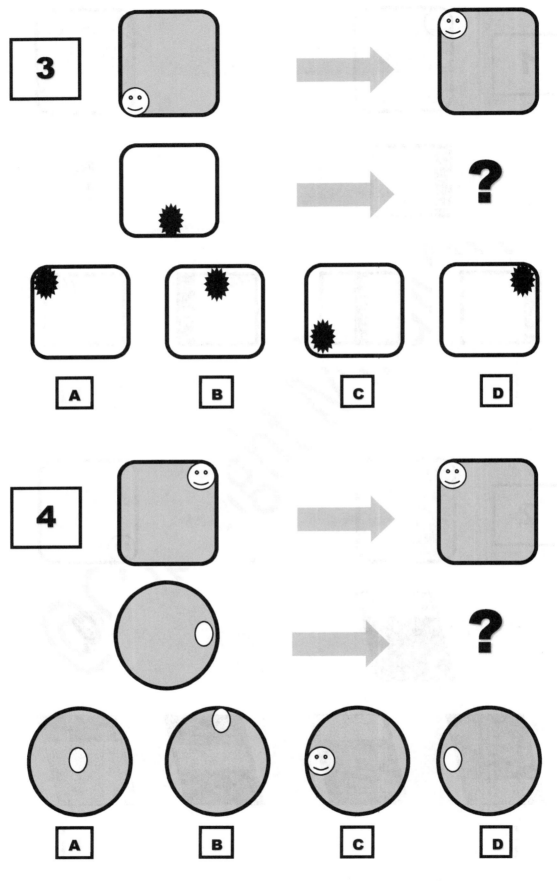

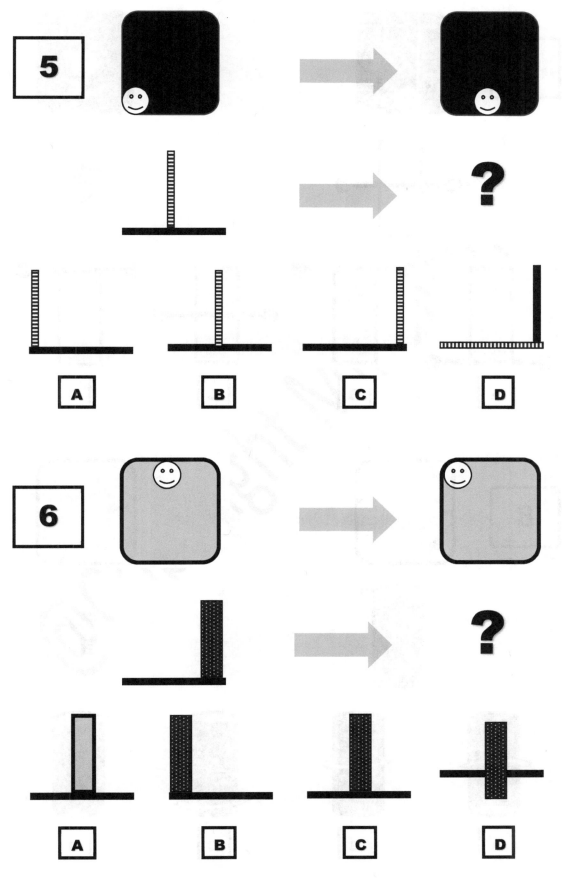

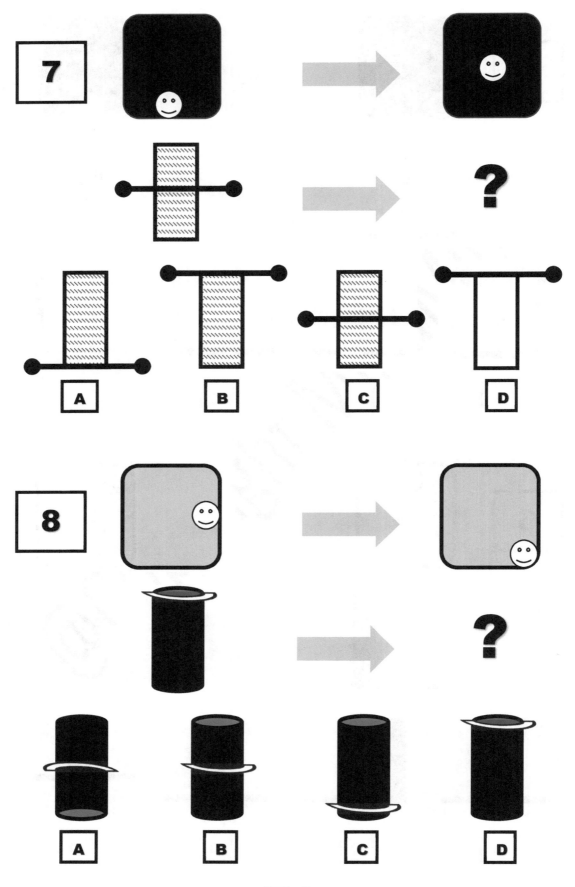

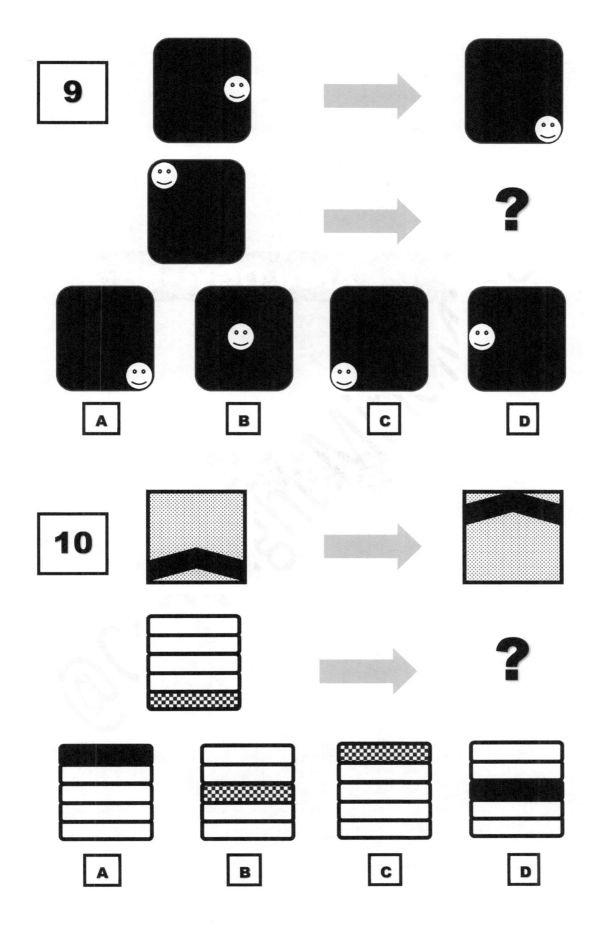

ANALOGY

SWAP

SWAP POSITION
BRING FRONT/SEND BACK

SWAP
POSITION

SWAP POSITION
BRING FRONT/SEND BACK

SWAP
POSITION

SWAP POSITION

SWAP PLACE

SWAP
POSITION

SWAP COLOR

SWAP
COLOR

75

SWAP COLOR

SWAP
COLOR

SWAP POSITION
SWAP PLACE & SWAP COLOR

SWAP
POSITION

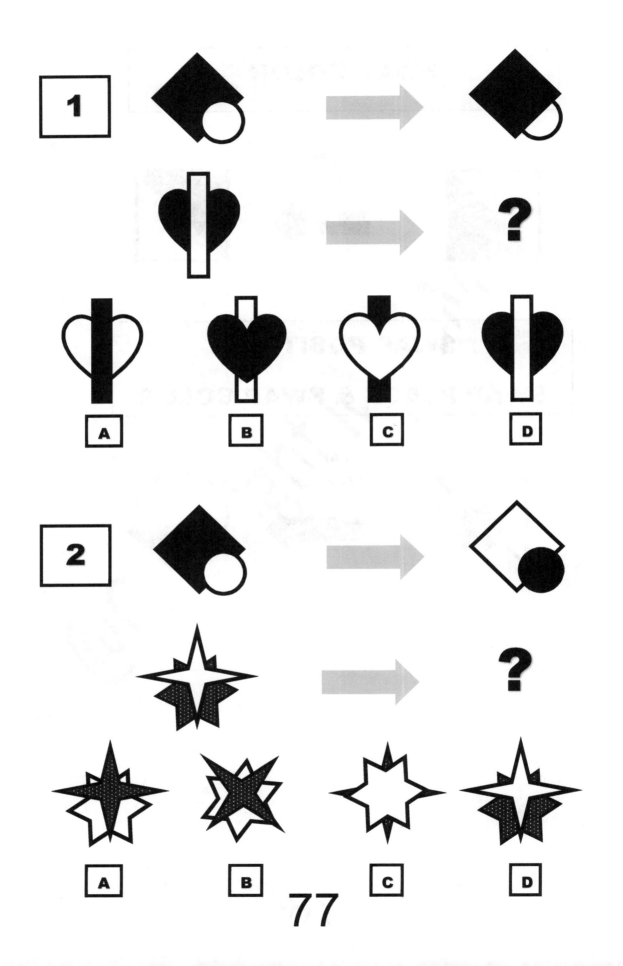

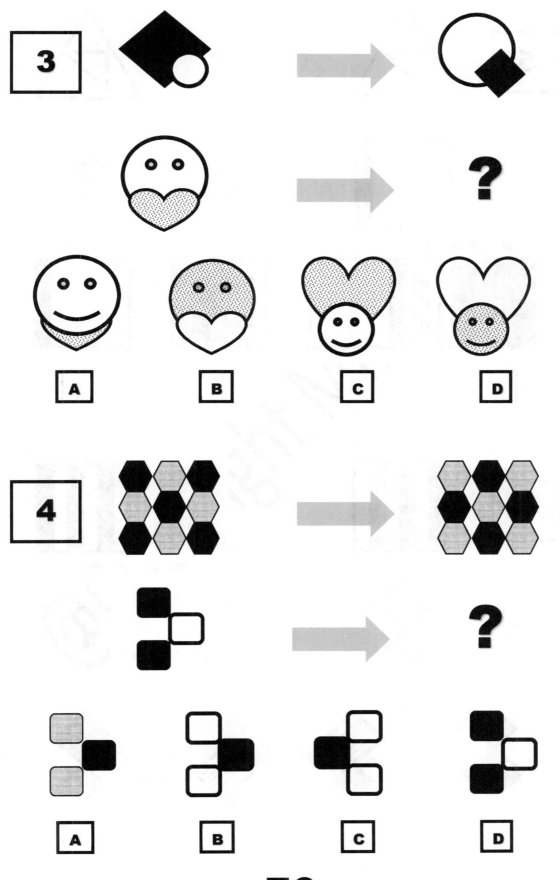

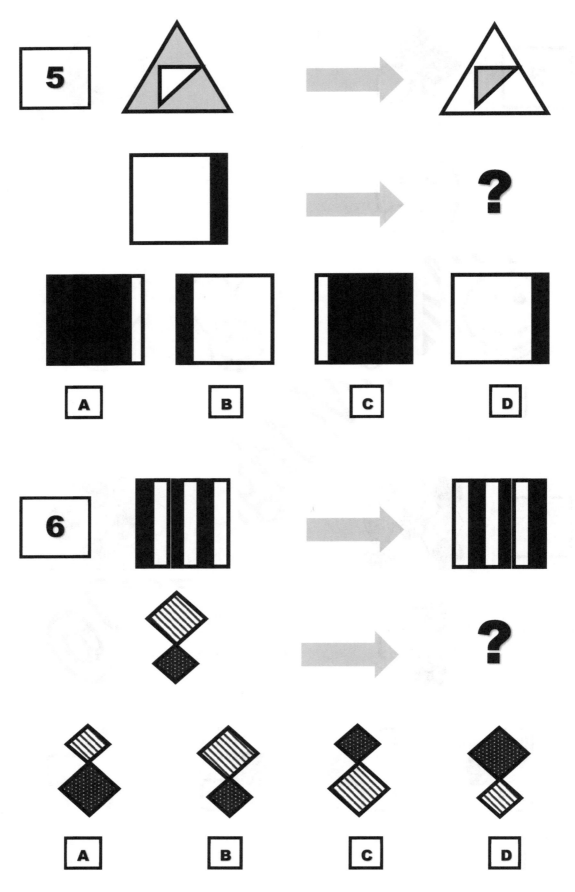

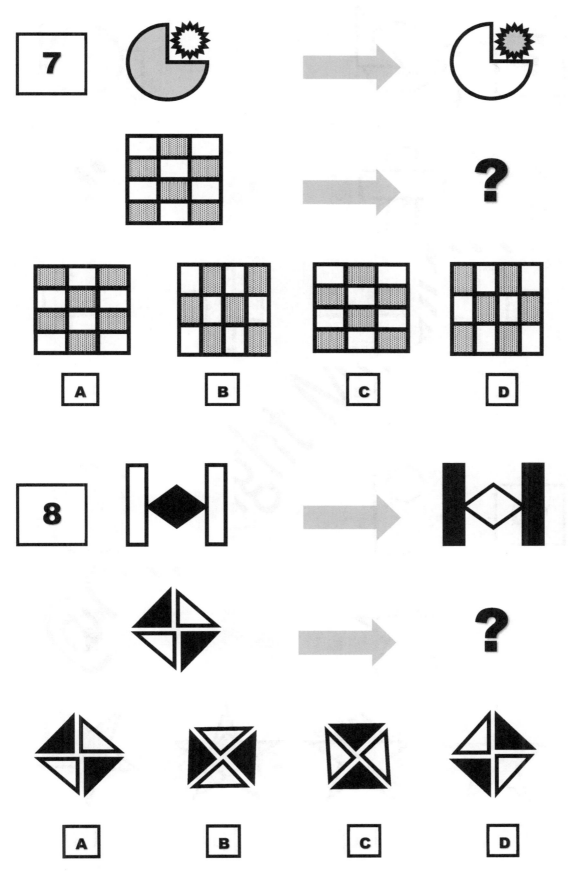

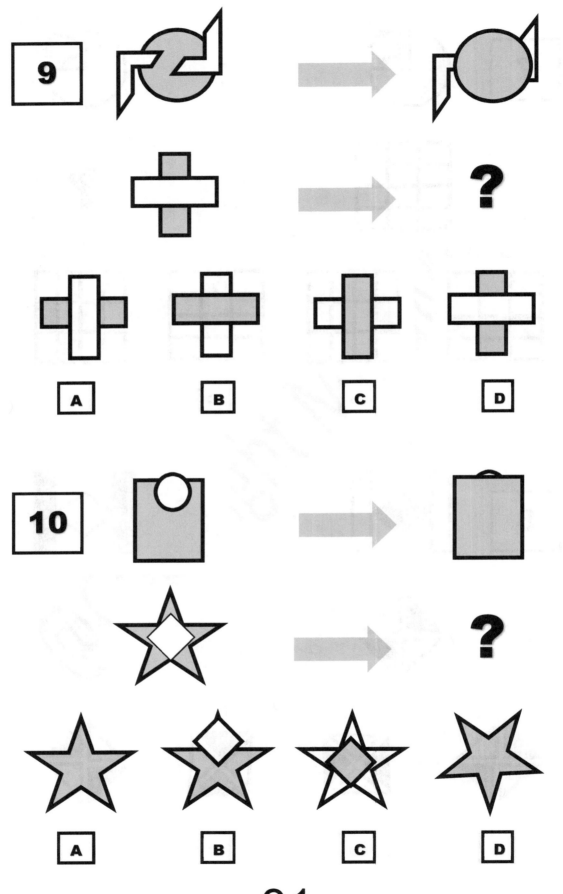

TURN
(ROTATE)

TURN CLOCKWISE

TURN CLOCKWISE

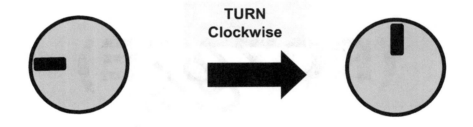

TURN CLOCKWISE

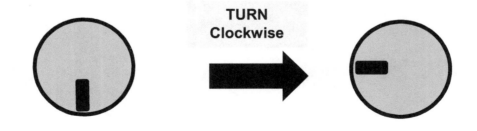

TURN COUNTER-CLOCKWISE

TURN COUNTER-CLOCKWISE

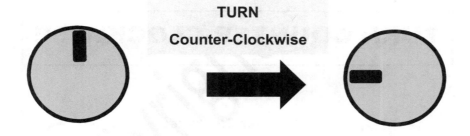

TURN COUNTER-CLOCKWISE

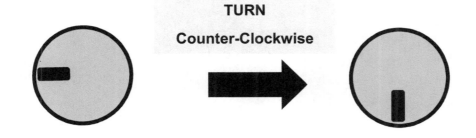

TURN CLOCKWISE

TURN COUNTER-CLOCKWISE

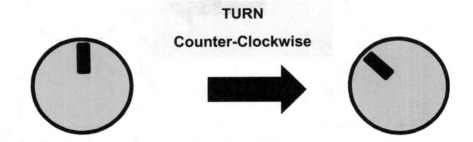

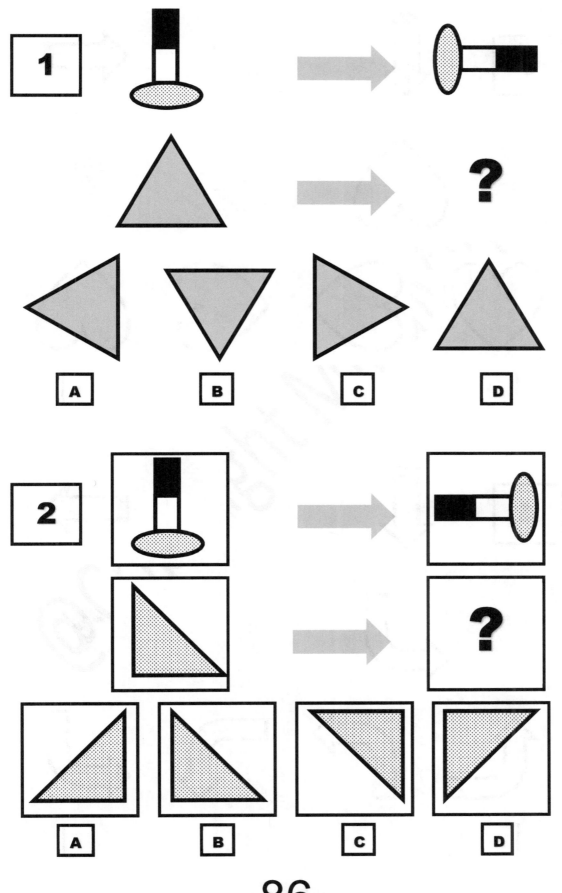

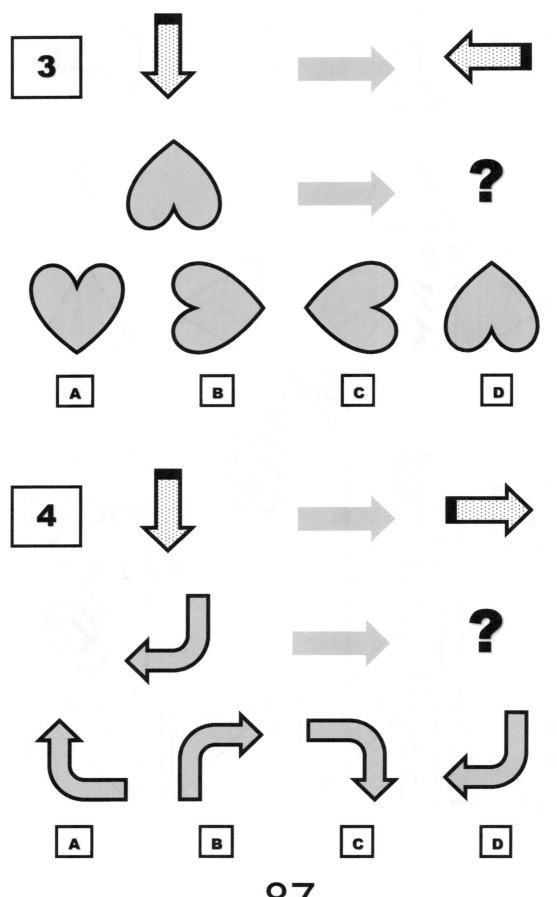

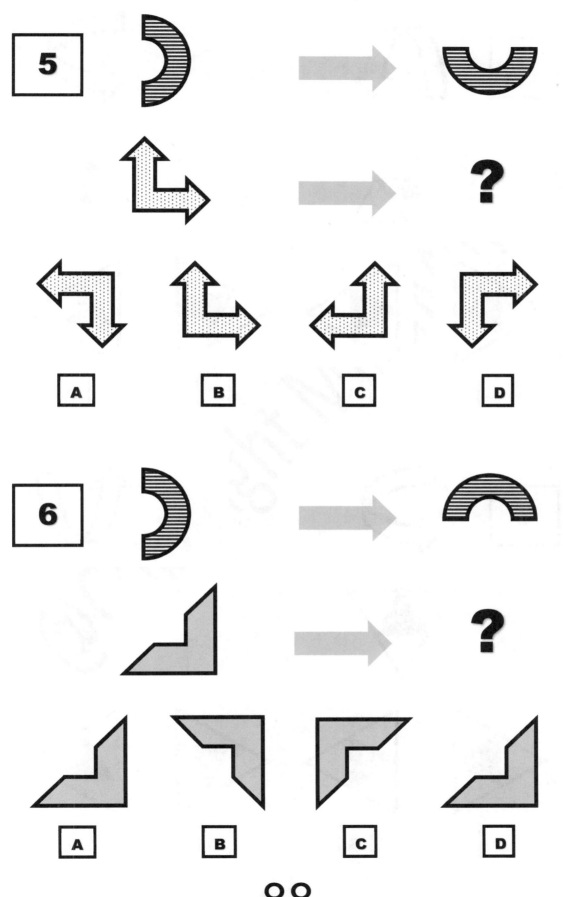

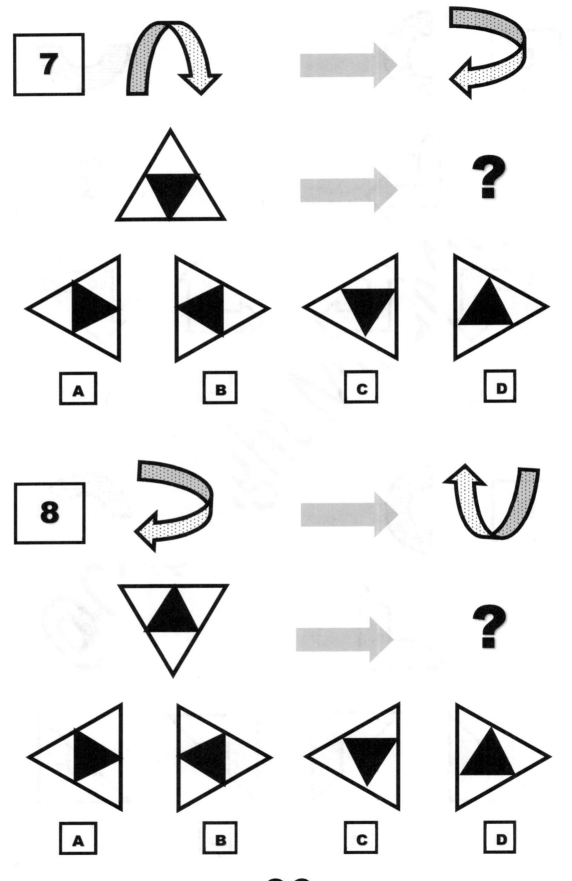

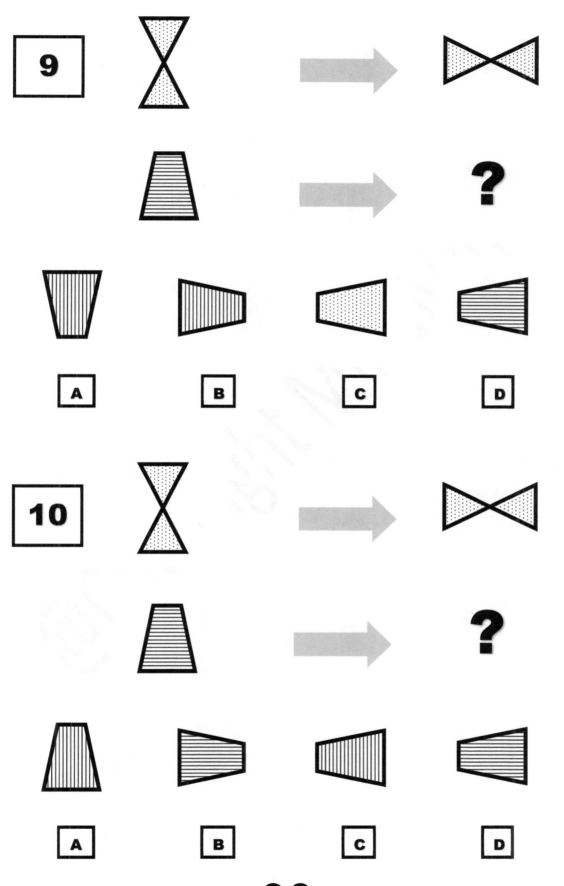

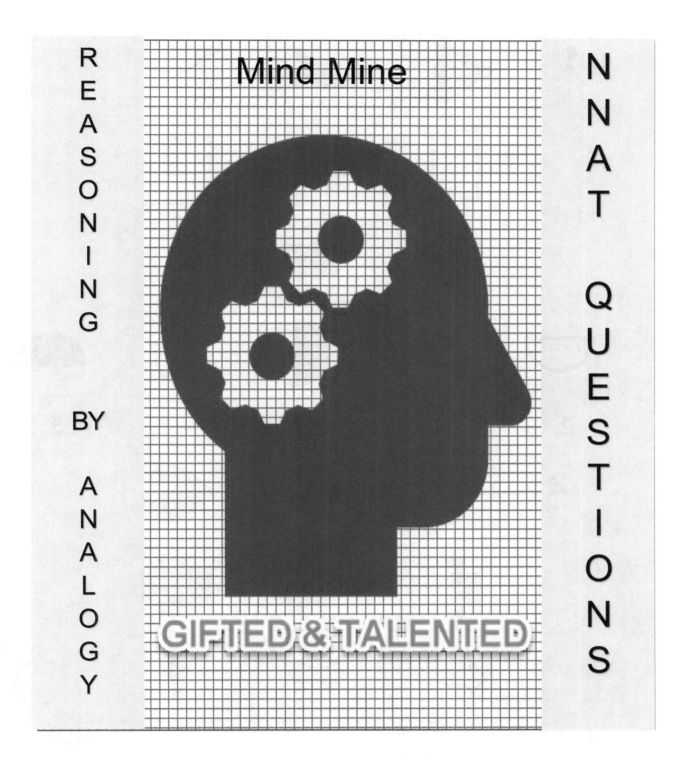

Mind Mine

GIFTED & TALENTED

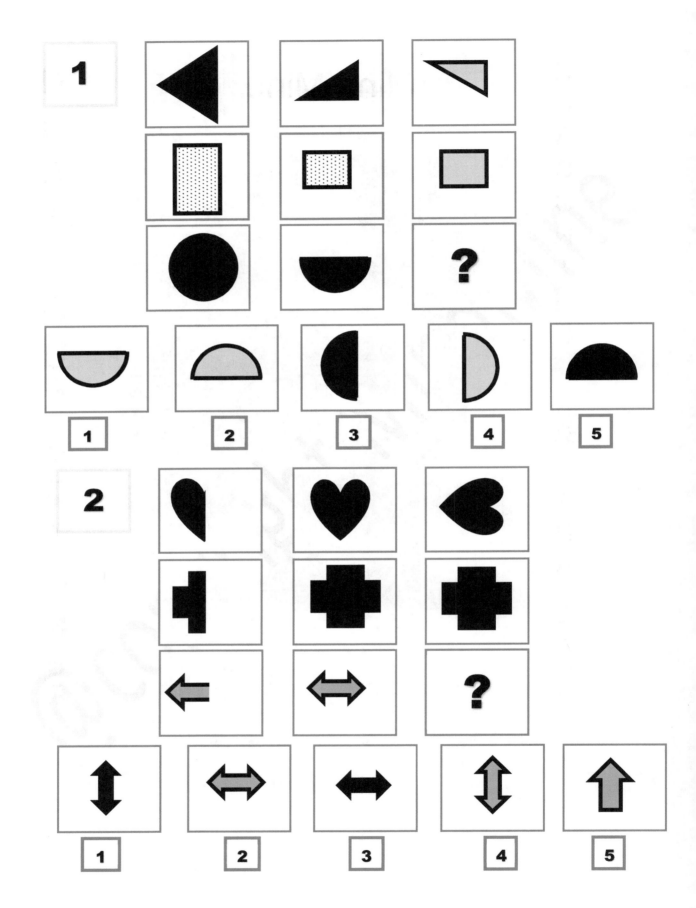

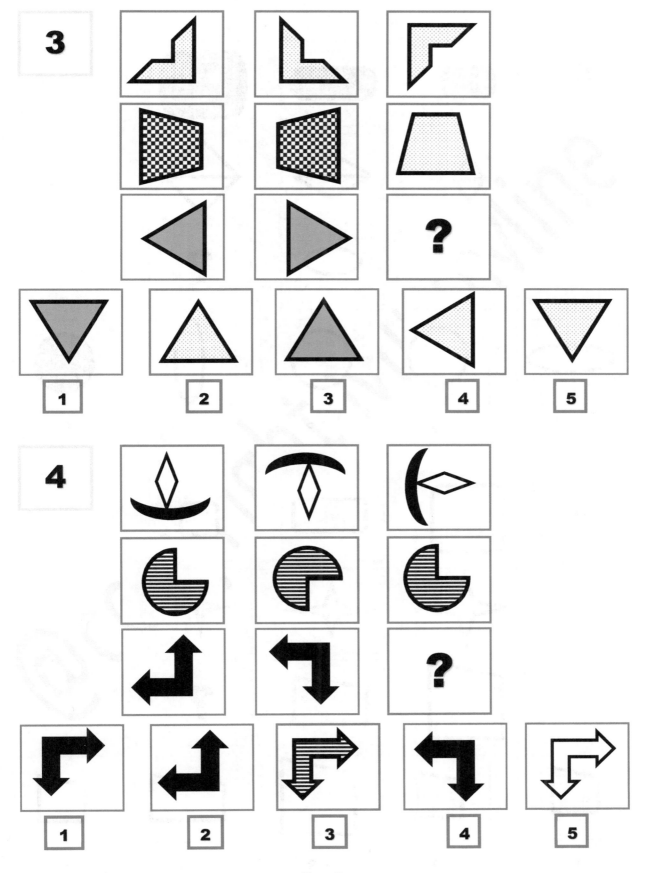

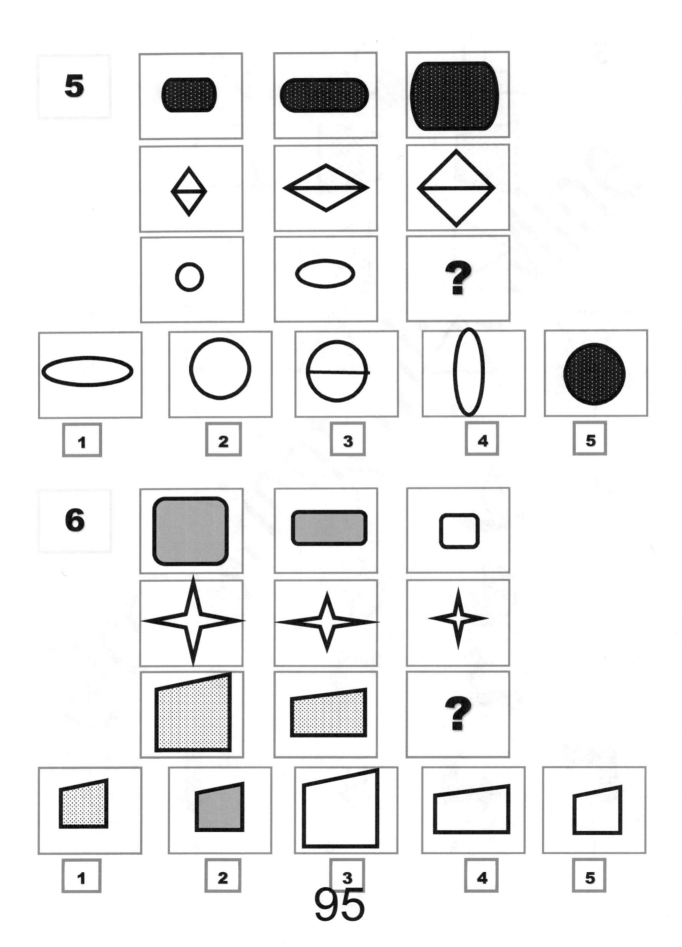

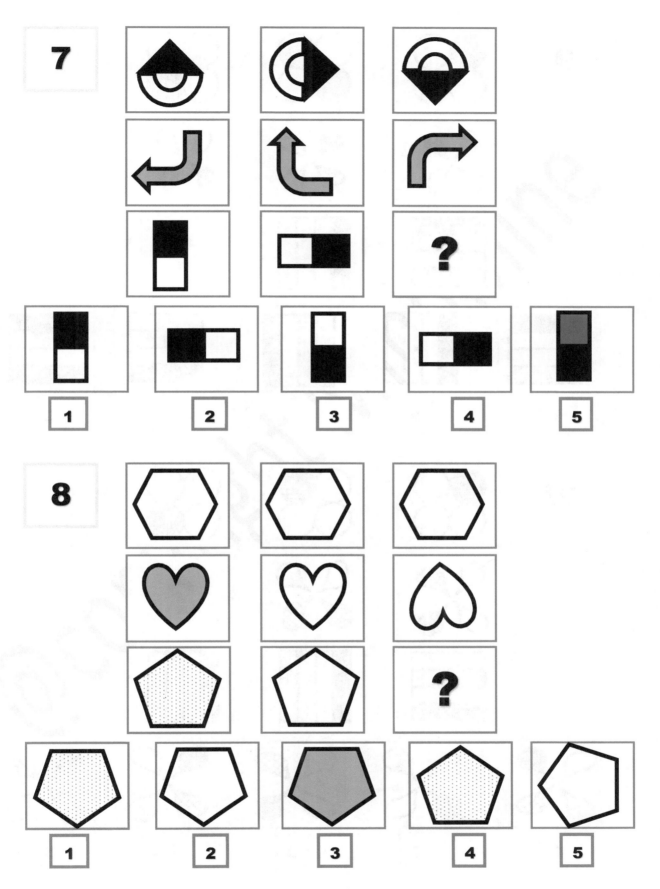

7

8

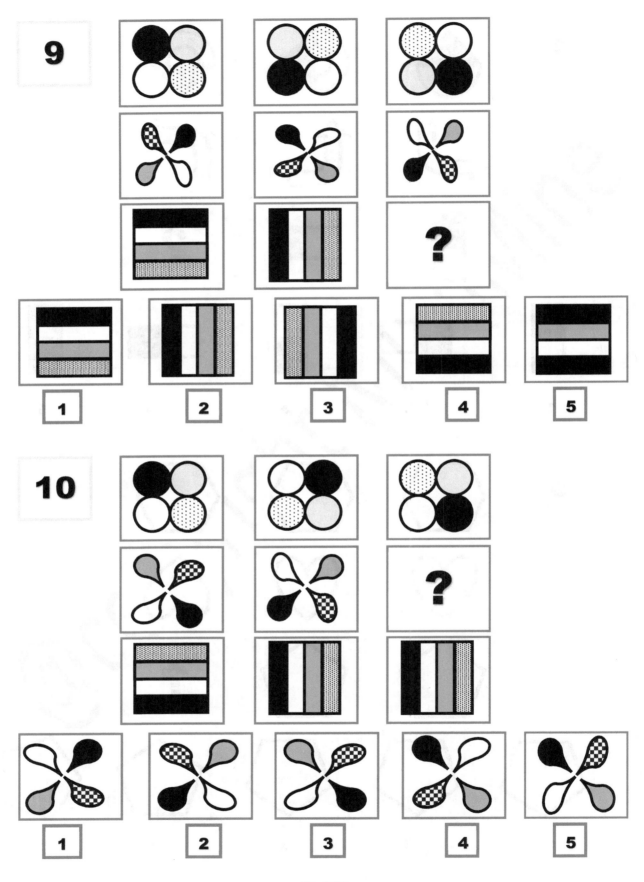

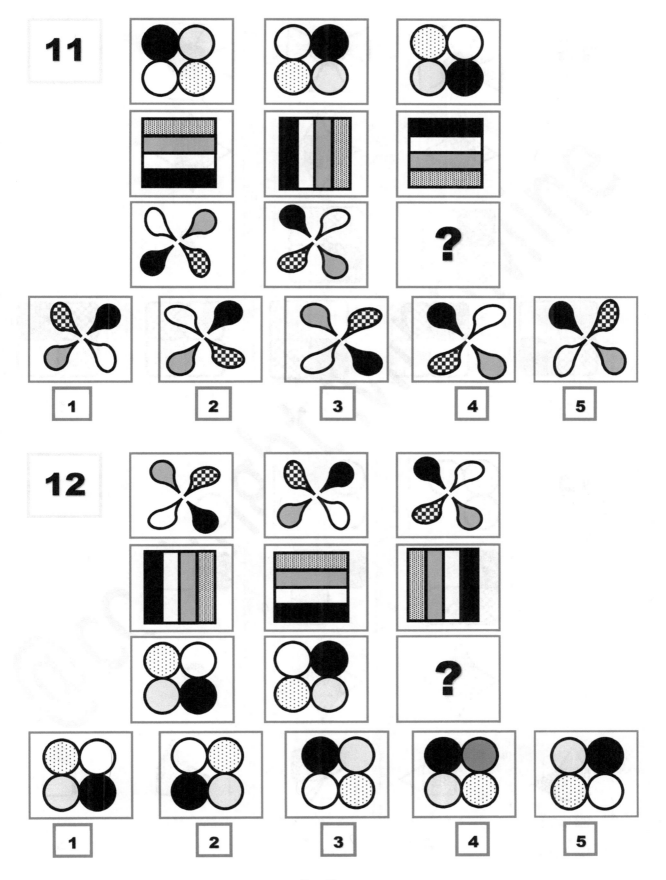

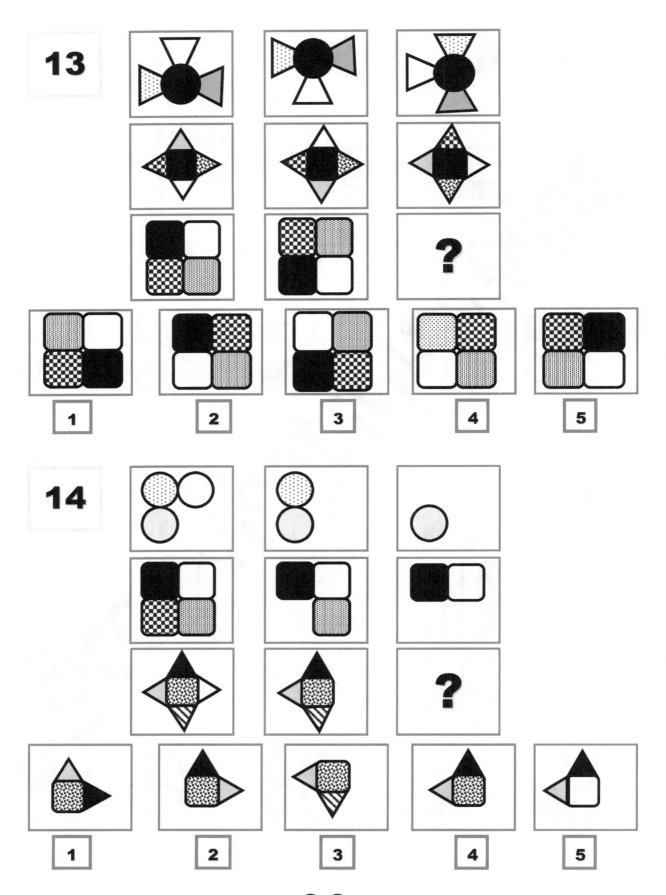

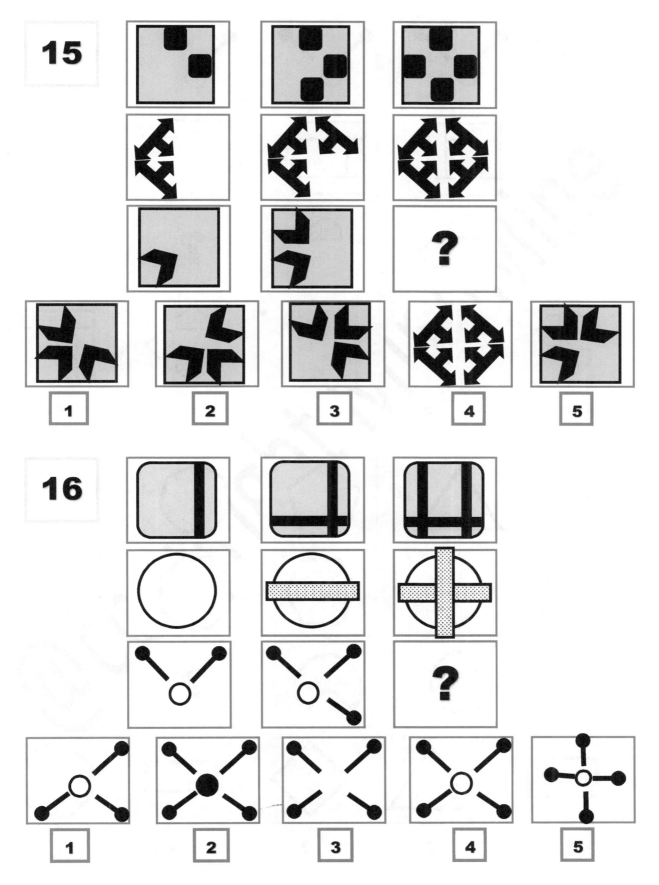

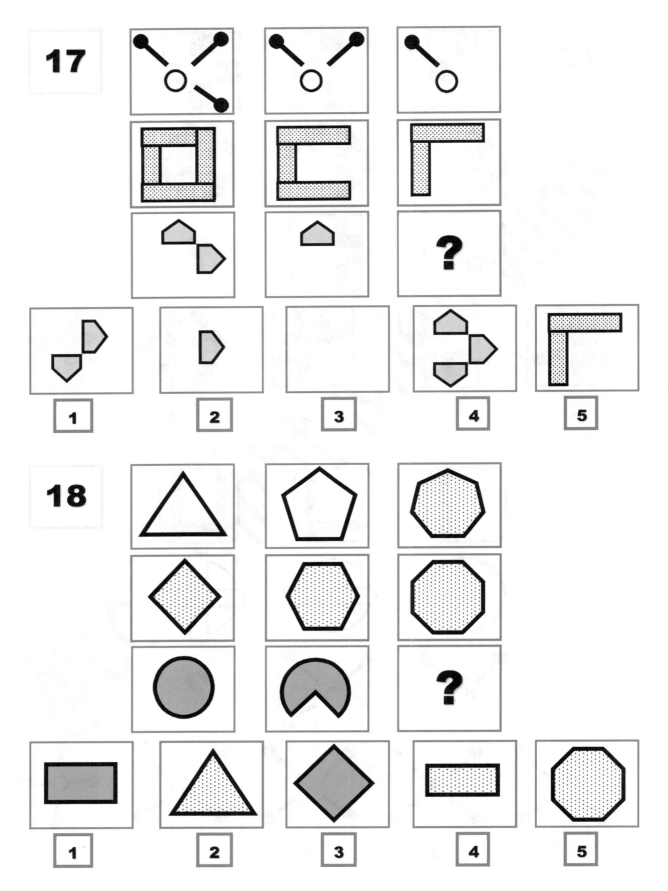

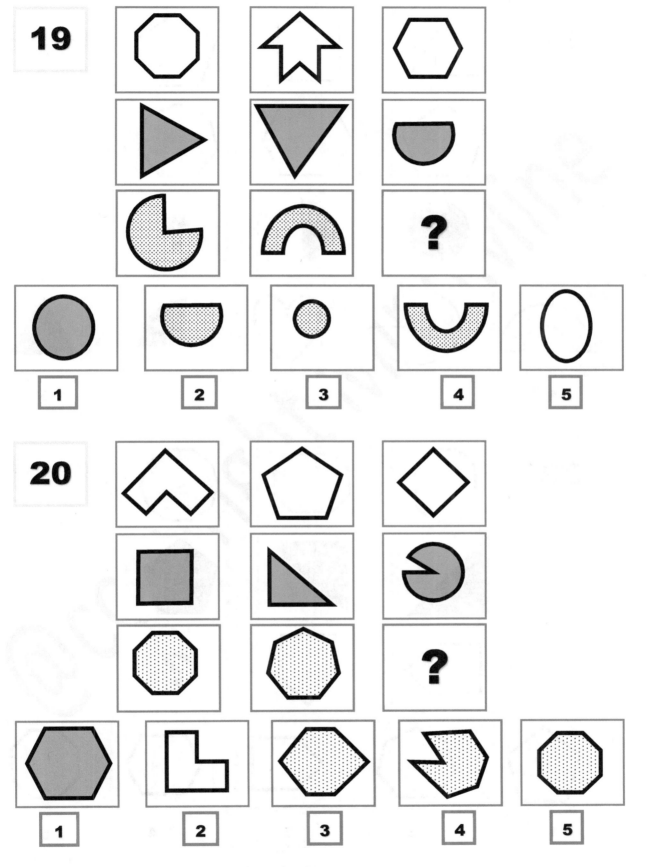

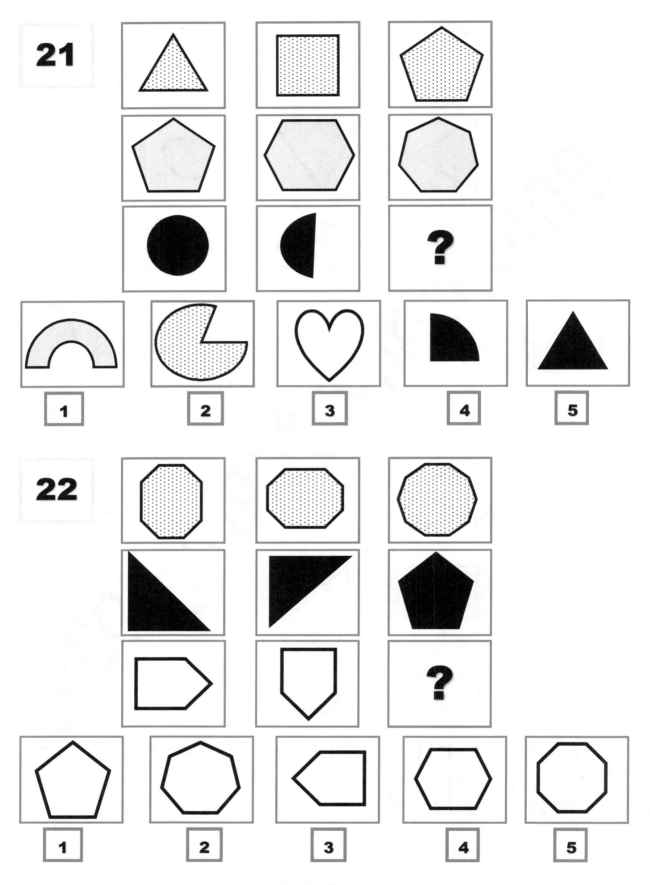

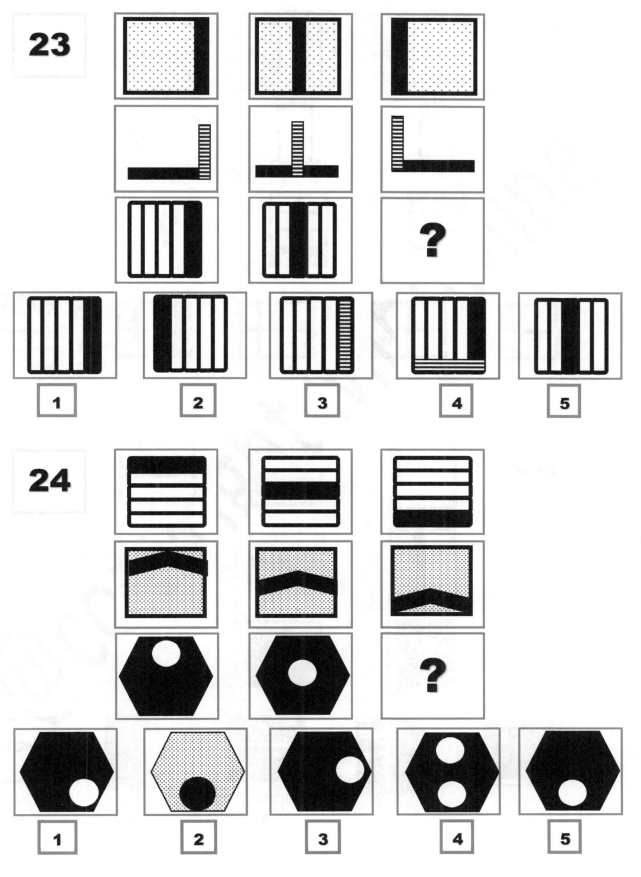

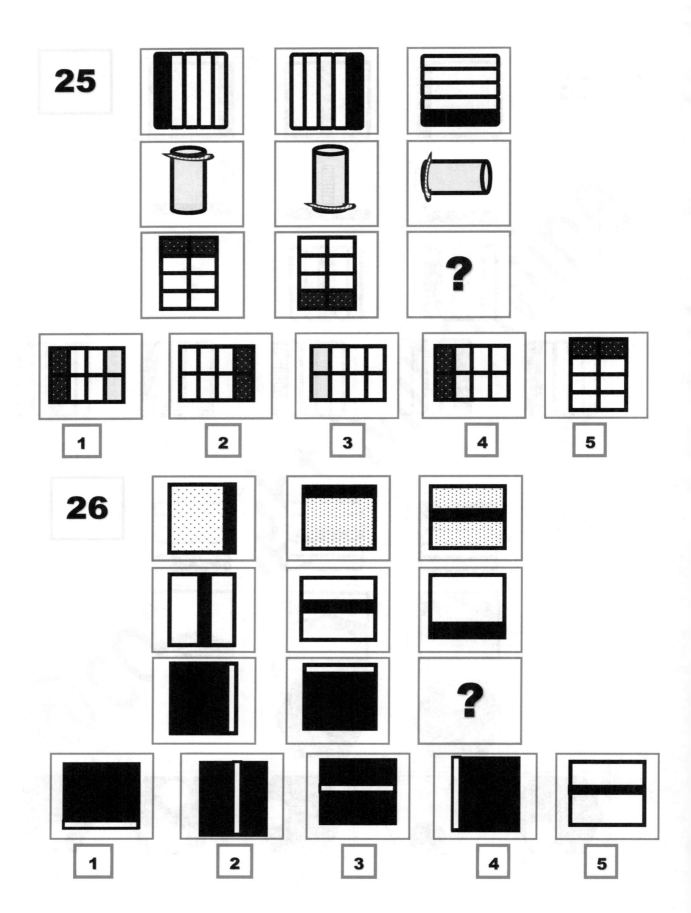

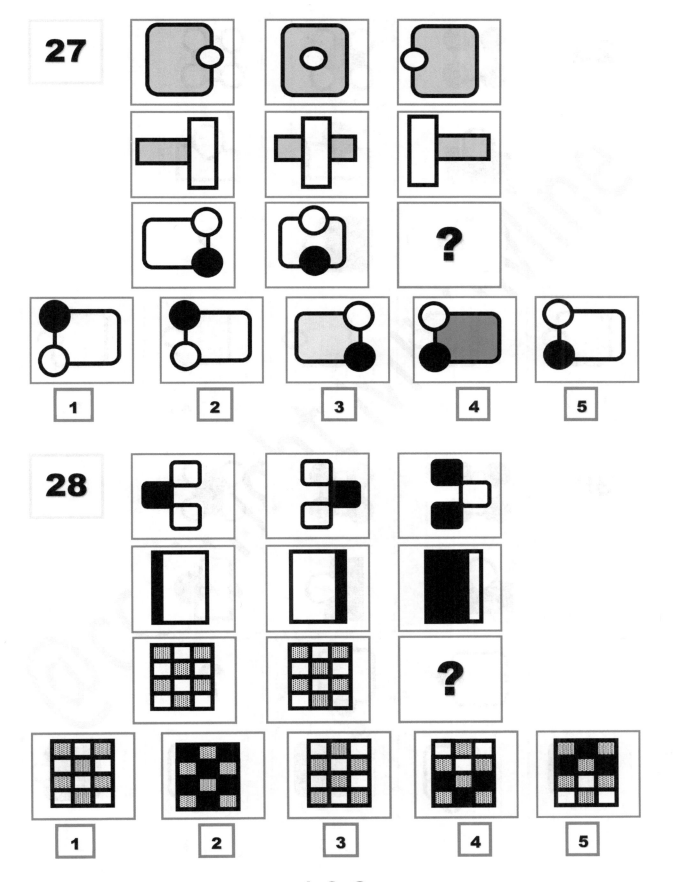

27

28

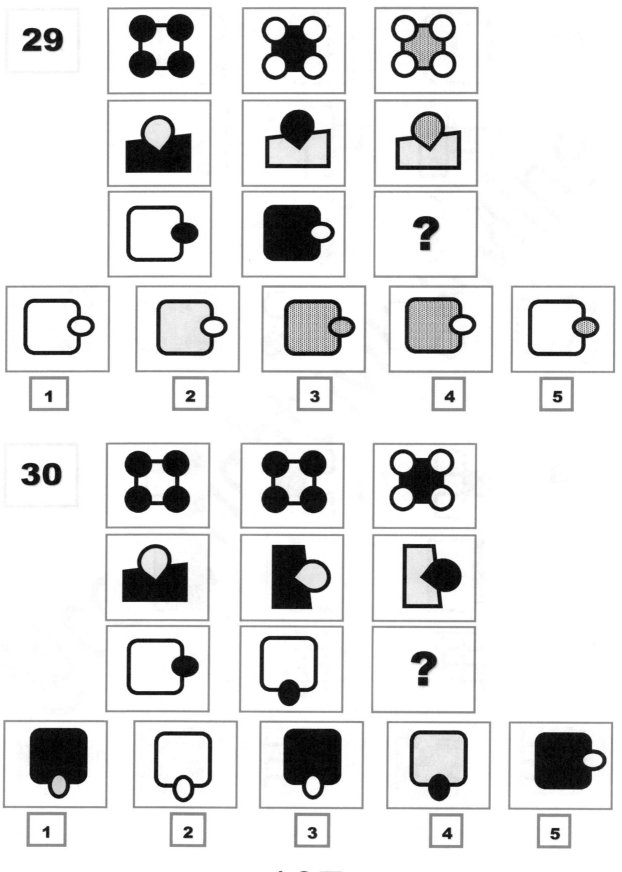

29

30

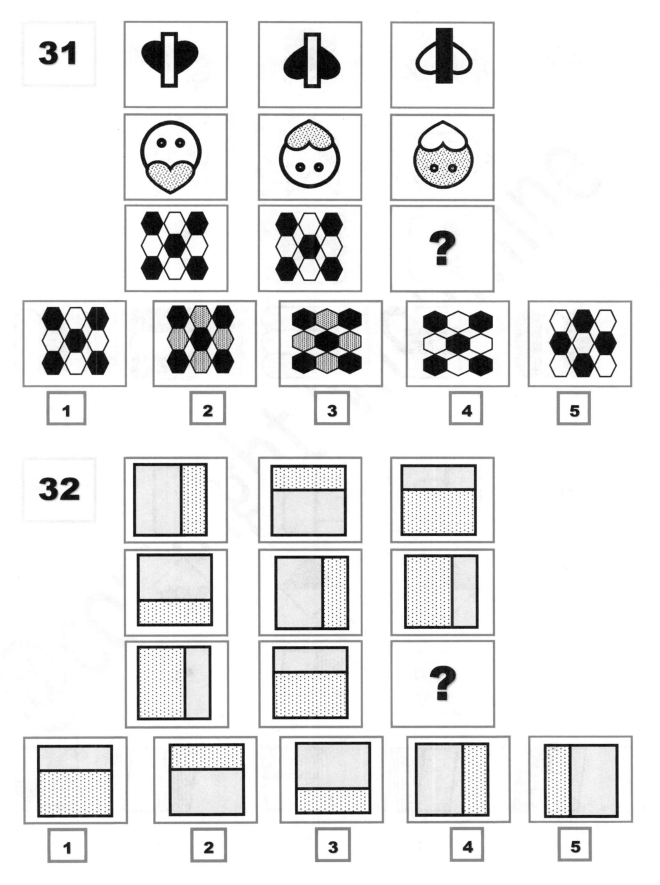

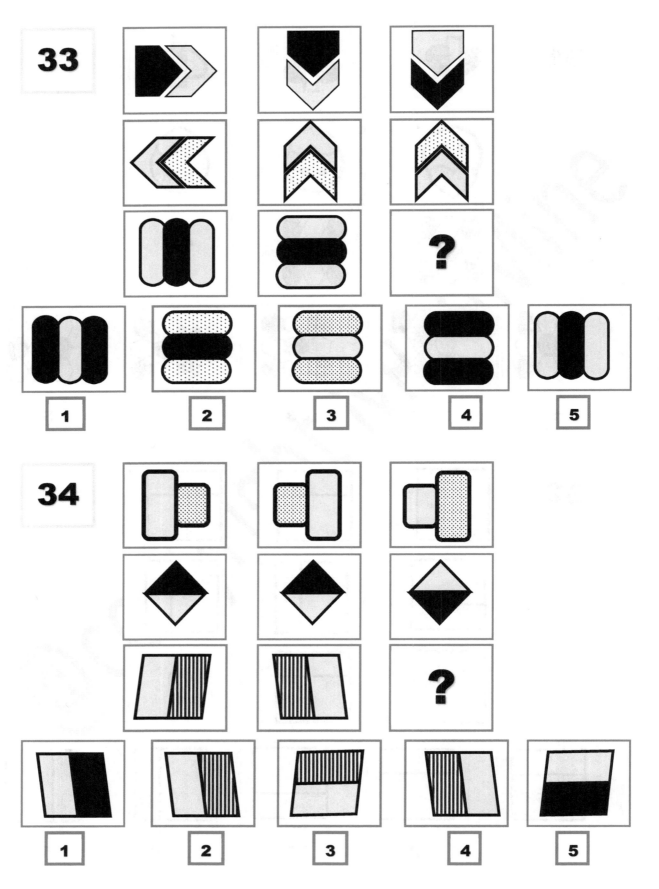

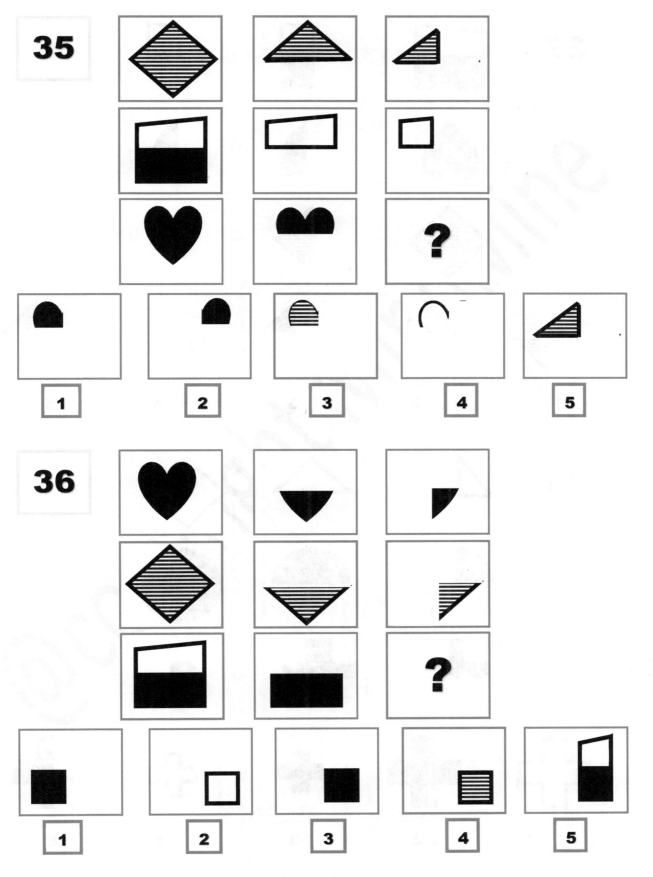

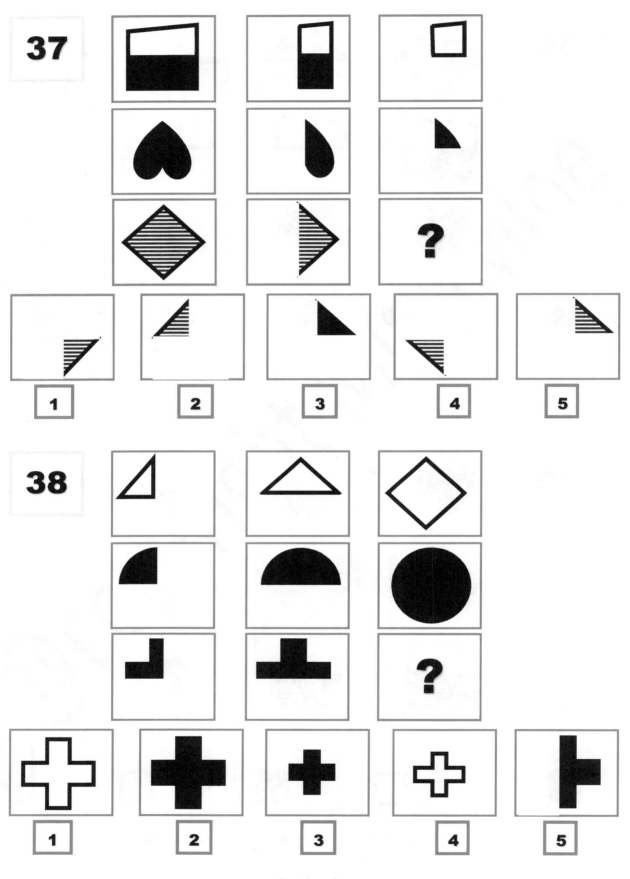

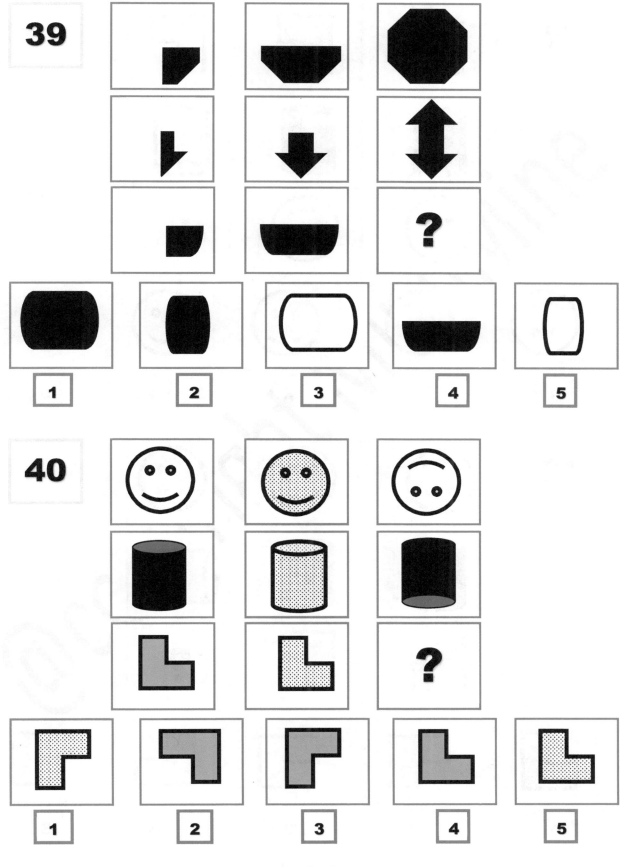

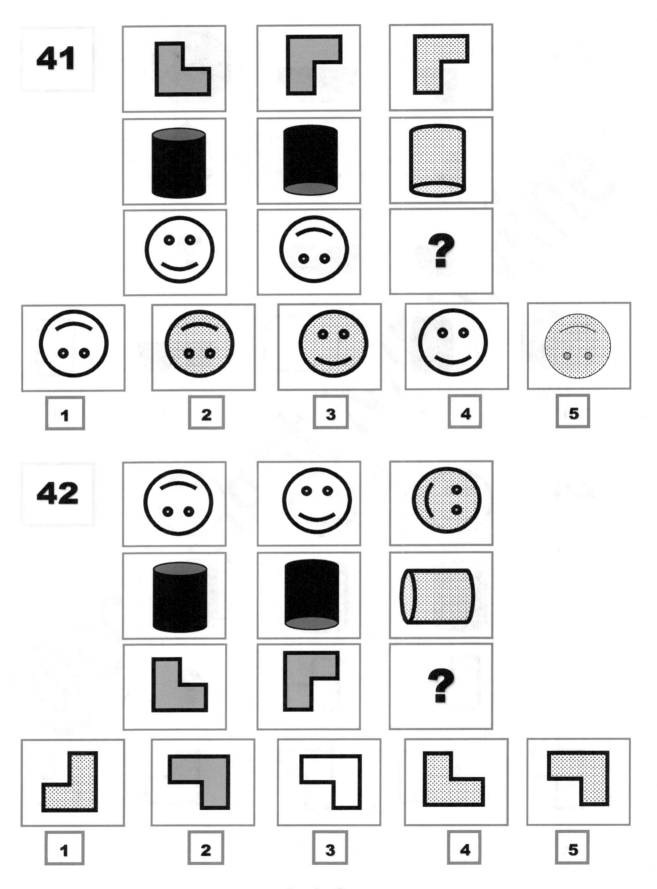

41

42

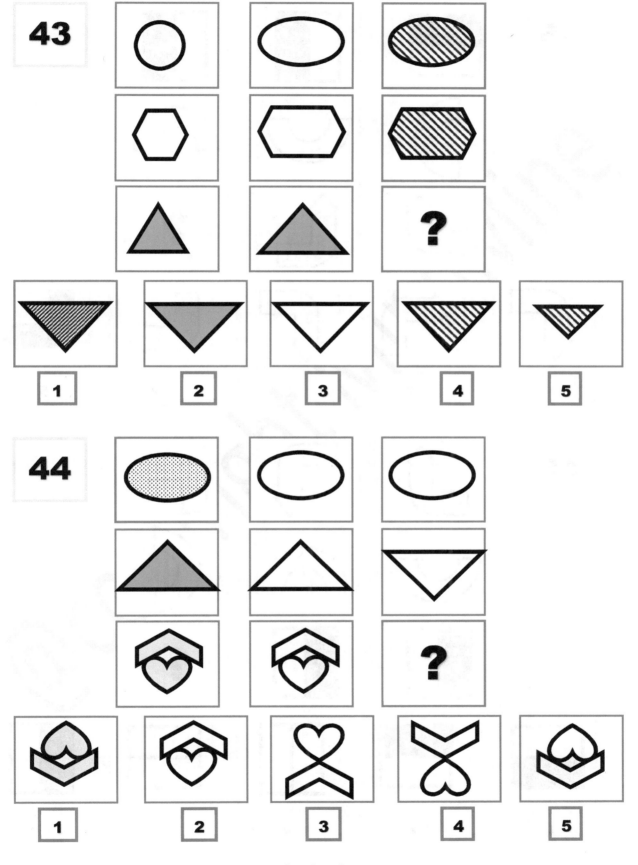

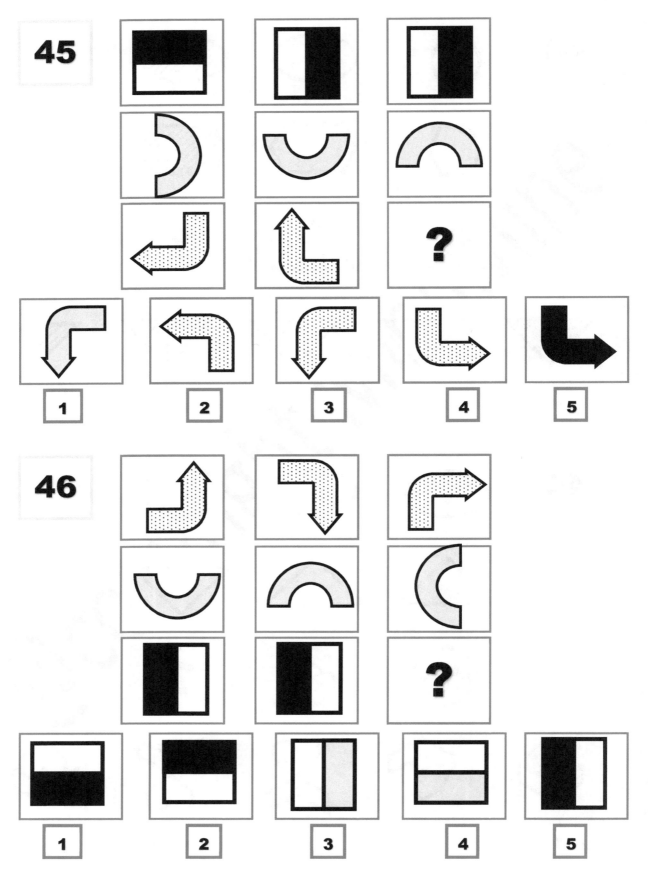

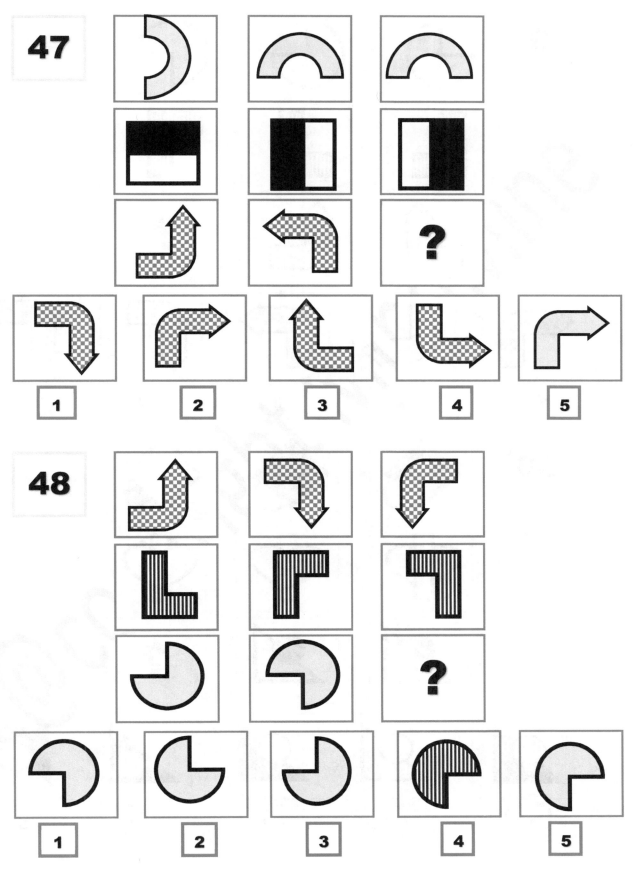

47

48

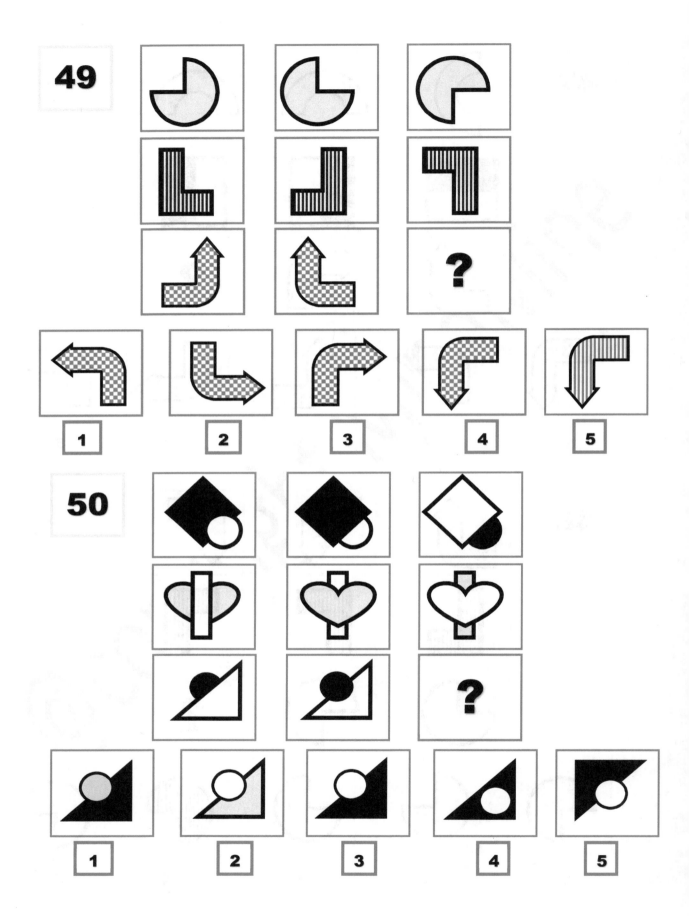

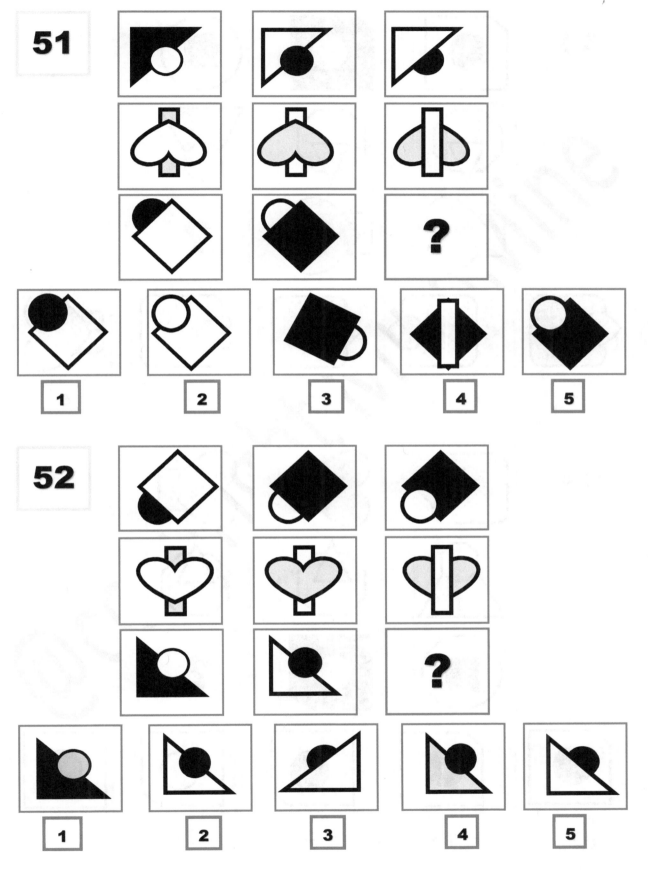

51

52

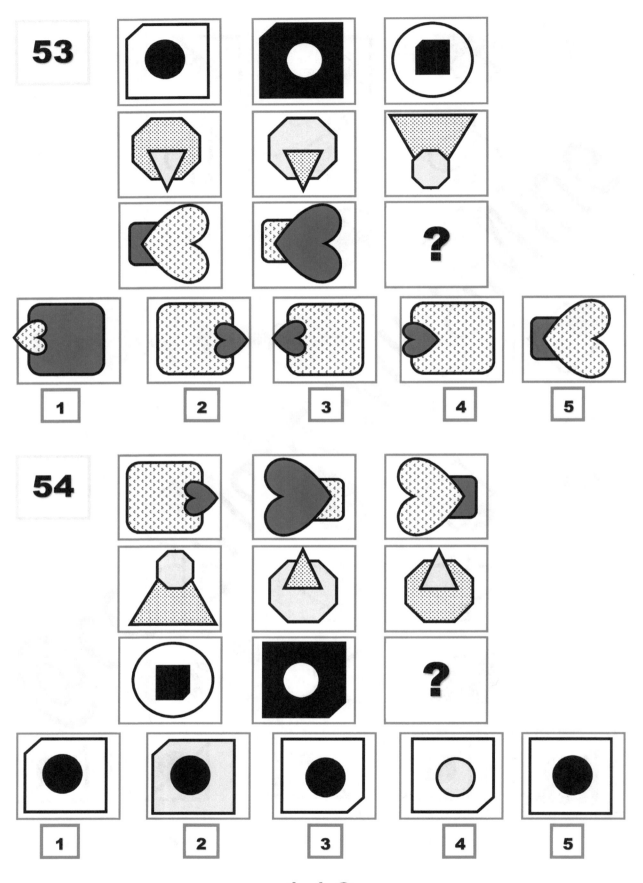

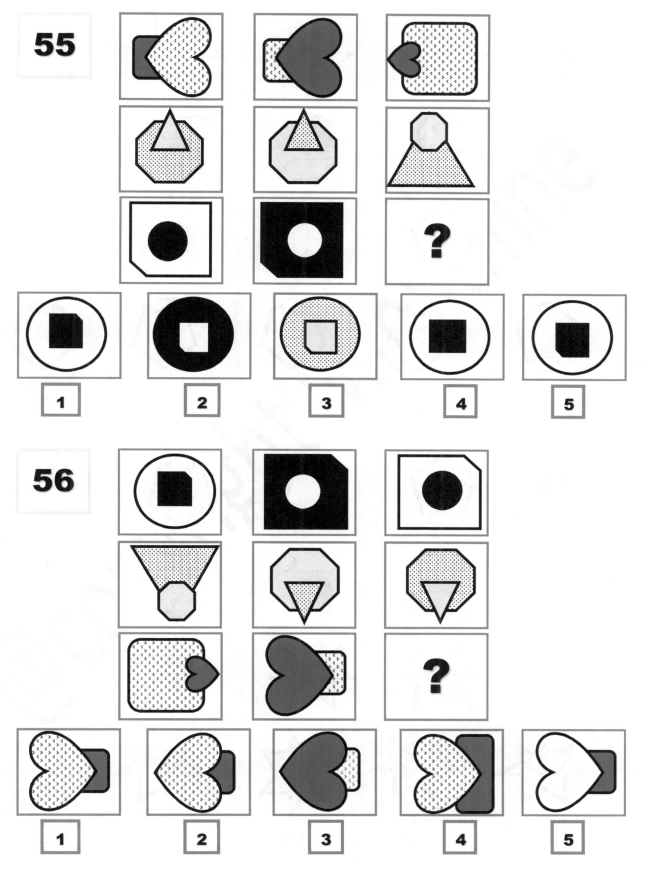

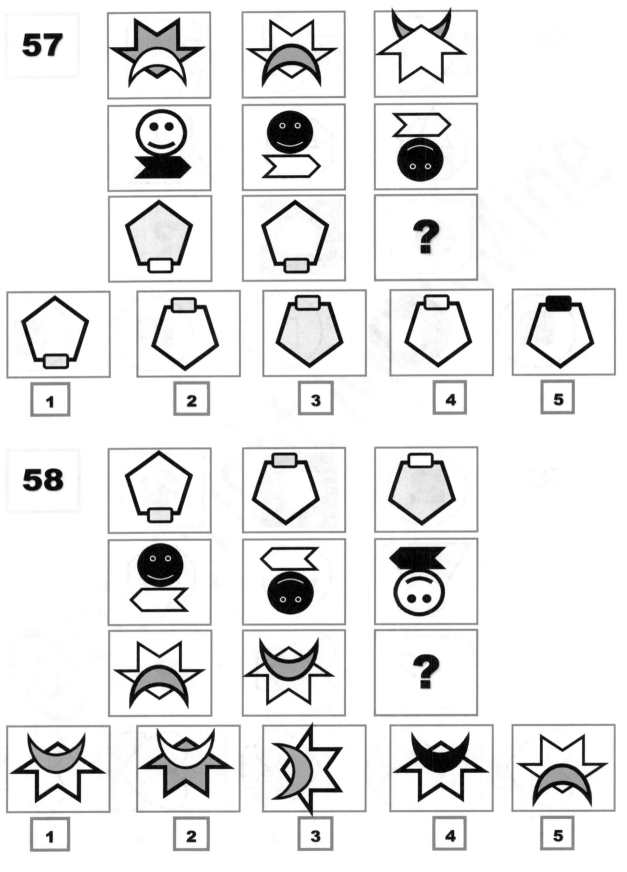

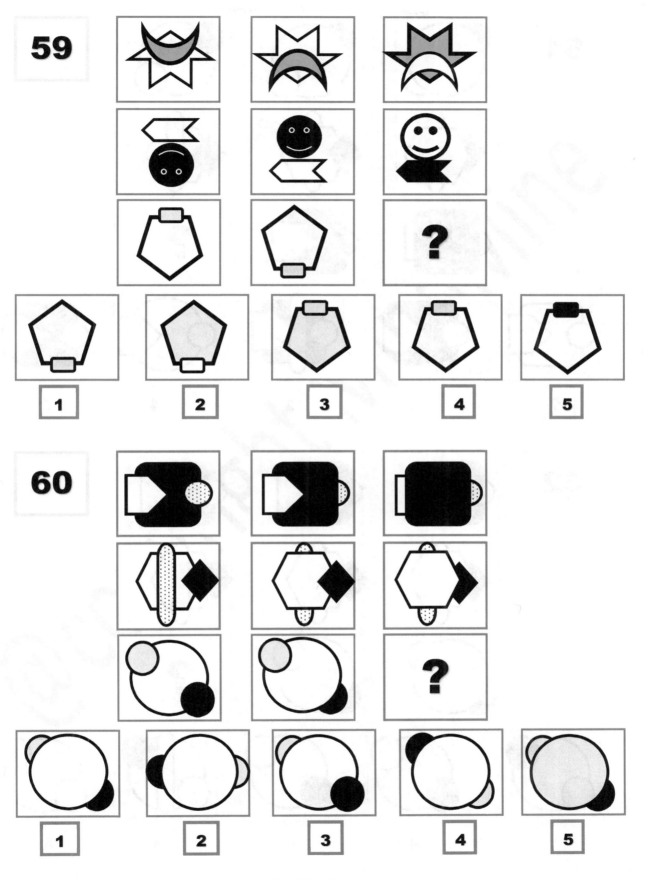

59

60

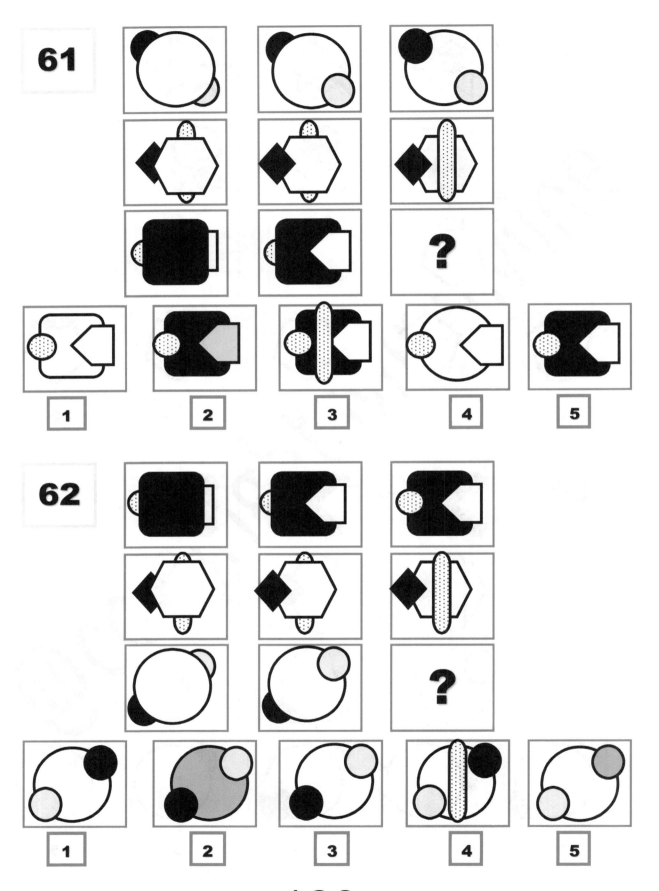

123

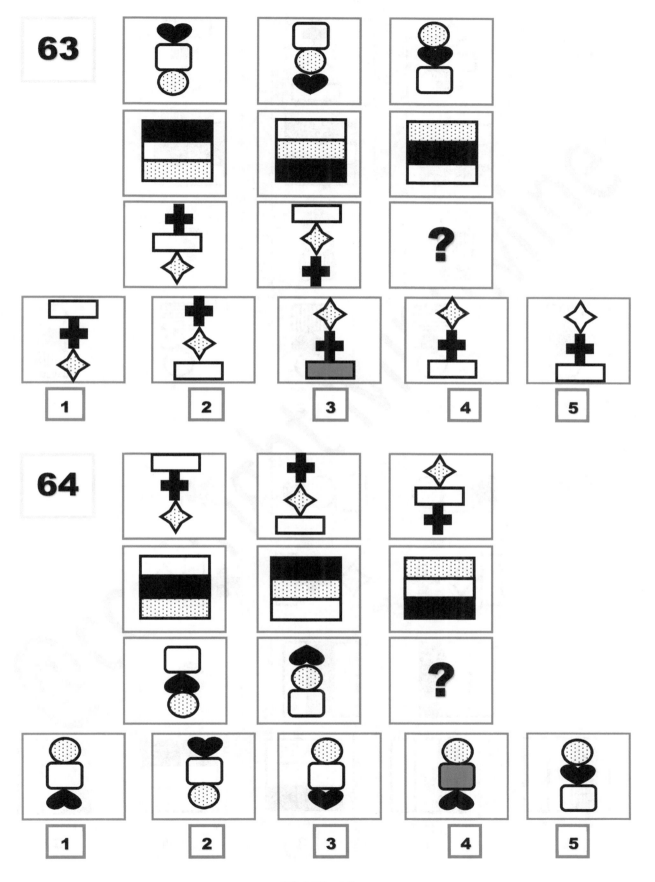

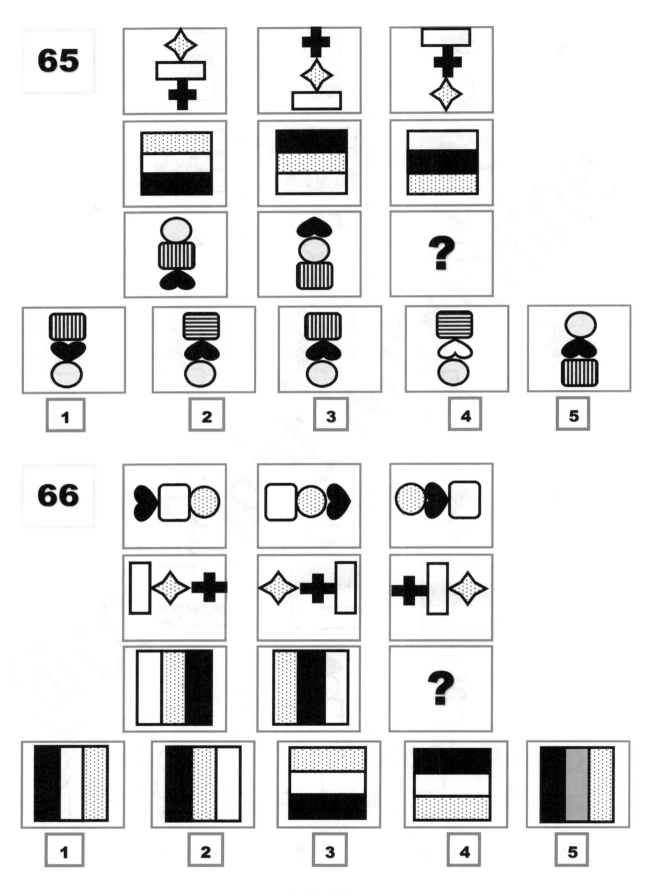

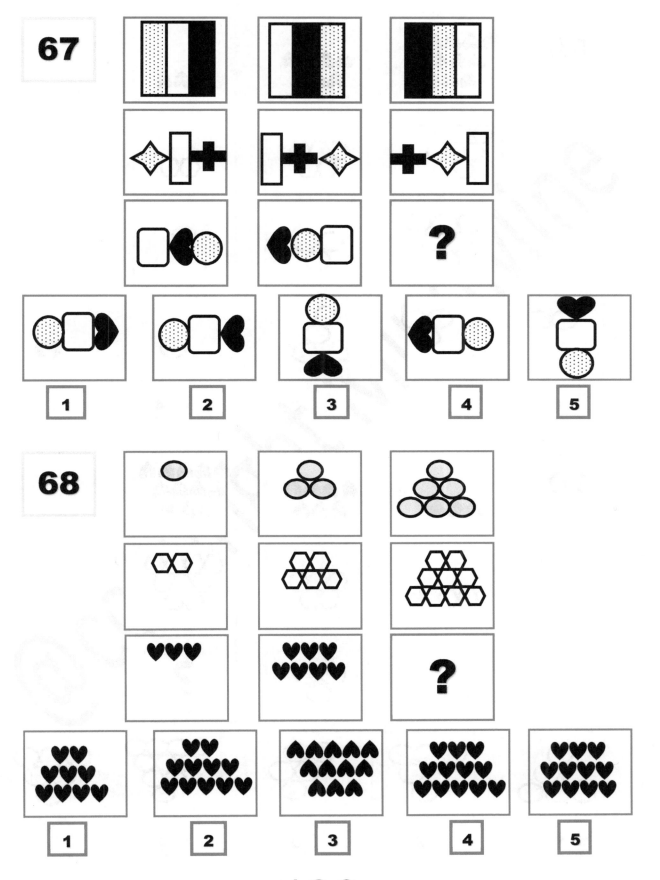

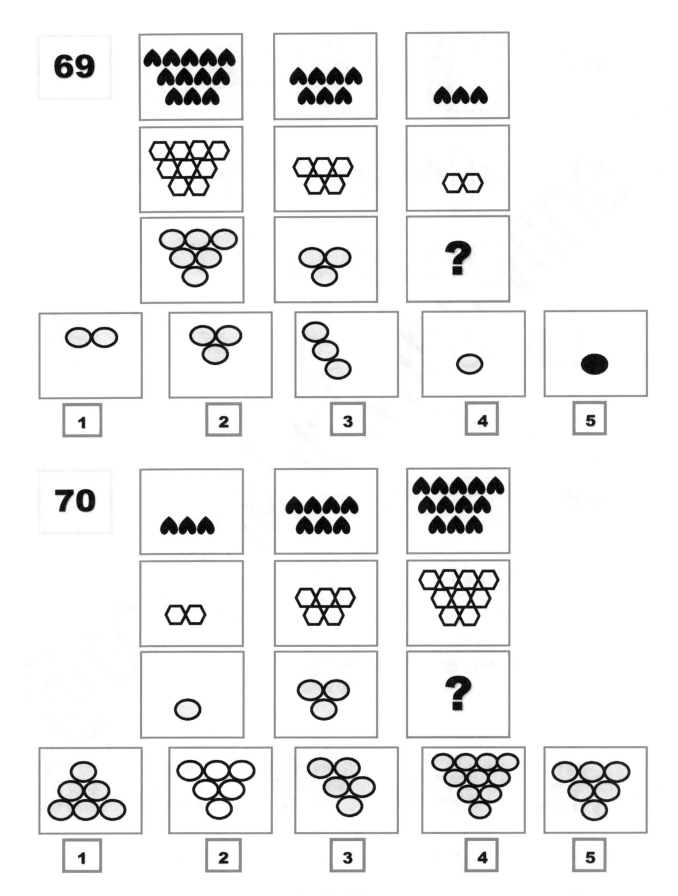

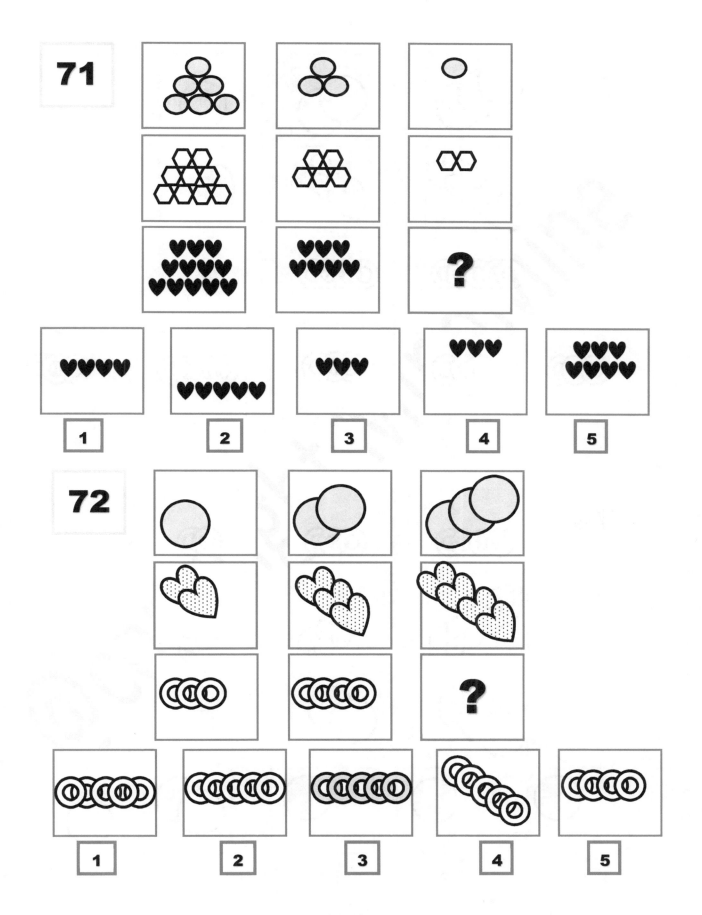

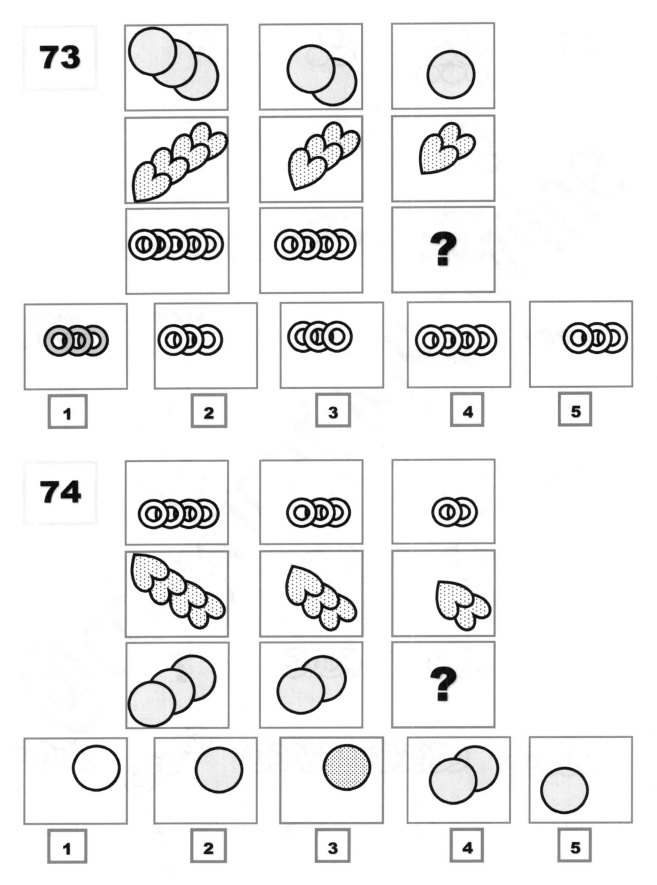

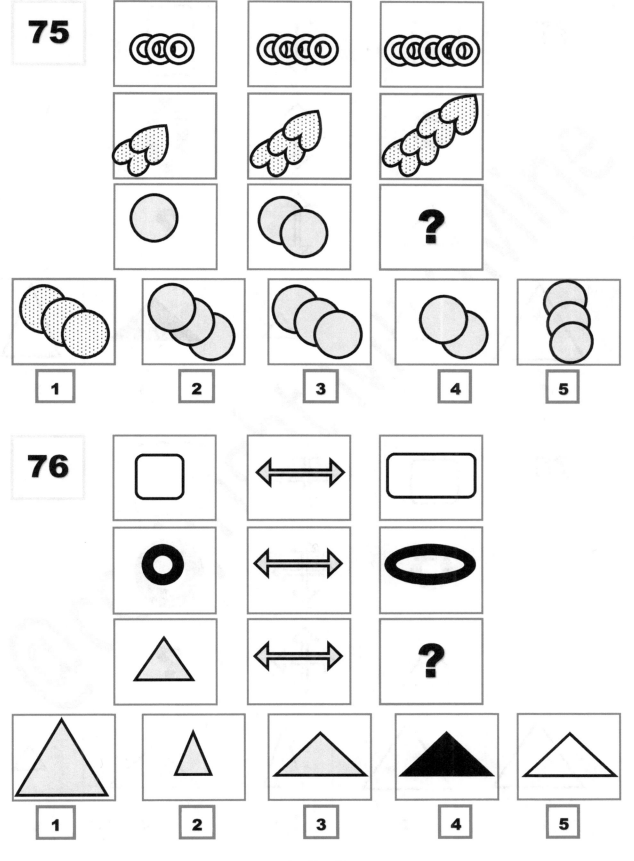

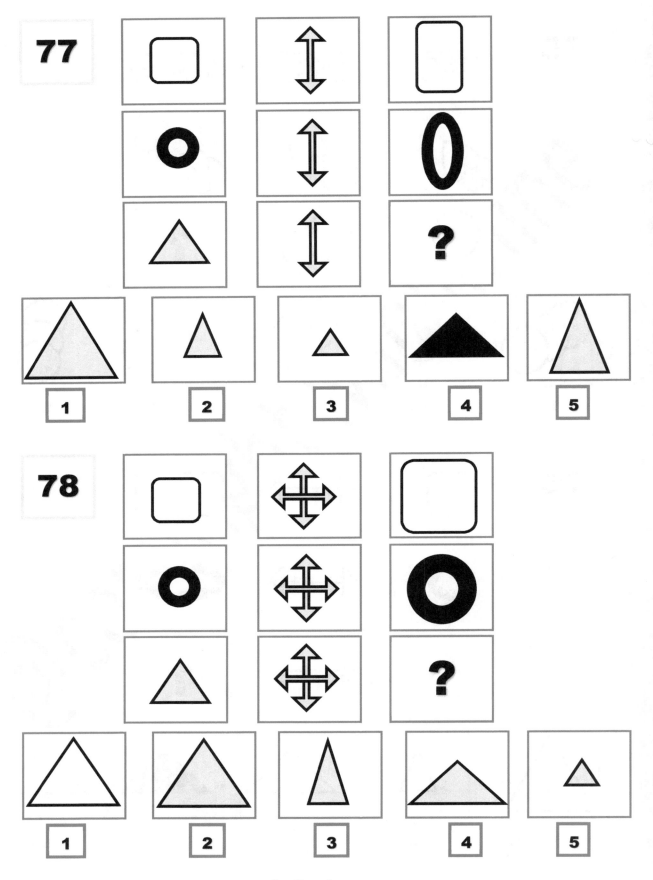

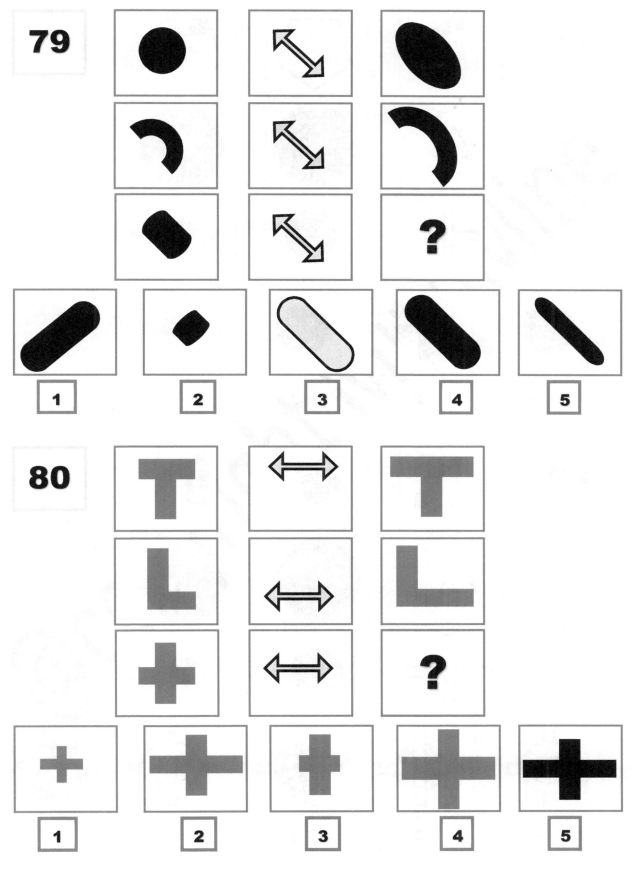

79

80

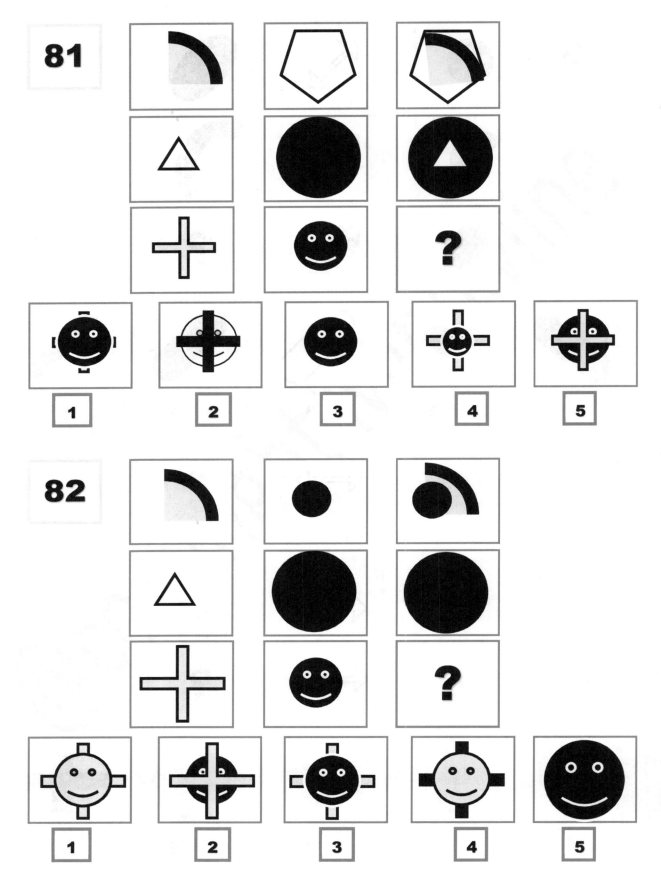

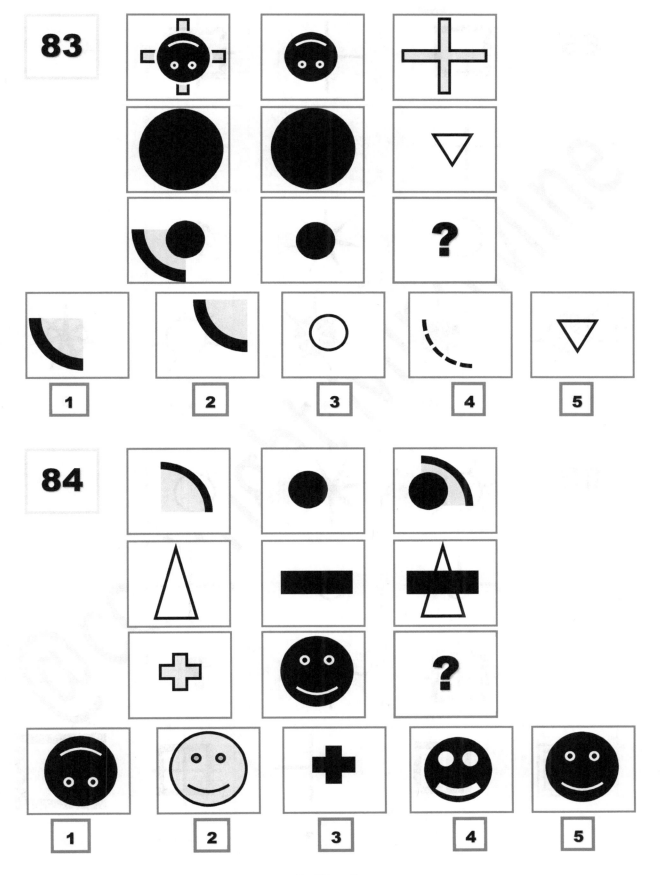

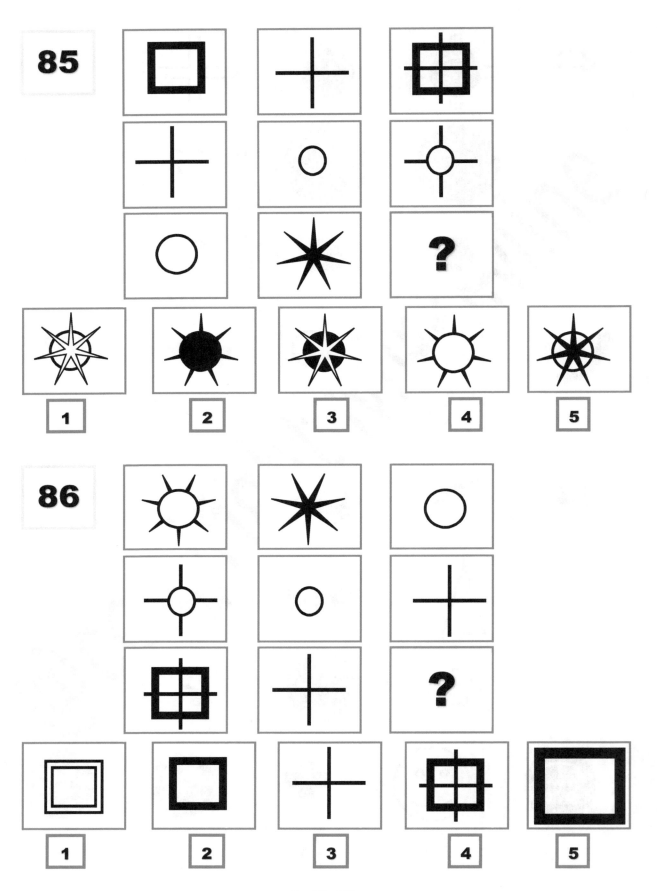

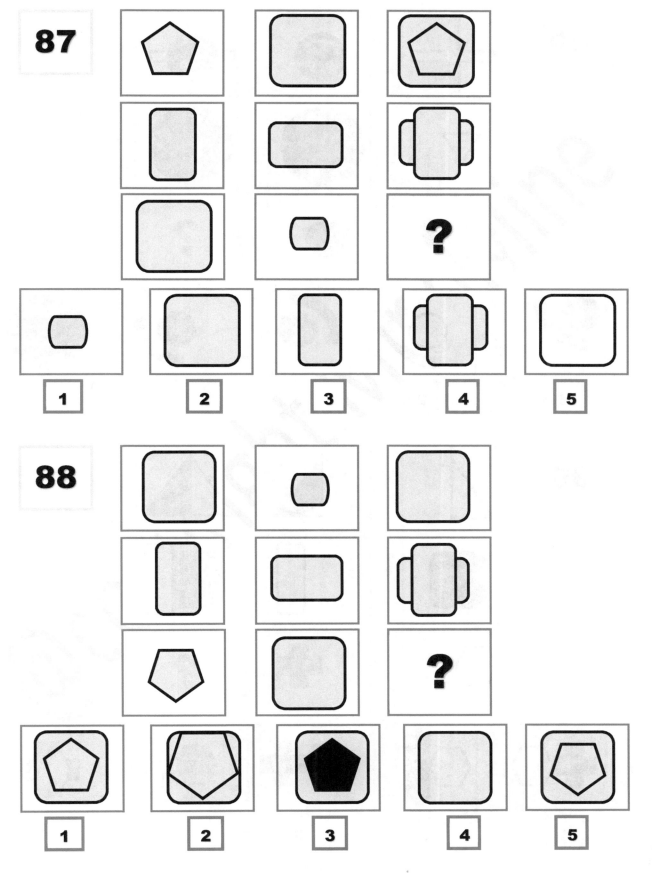

87

88

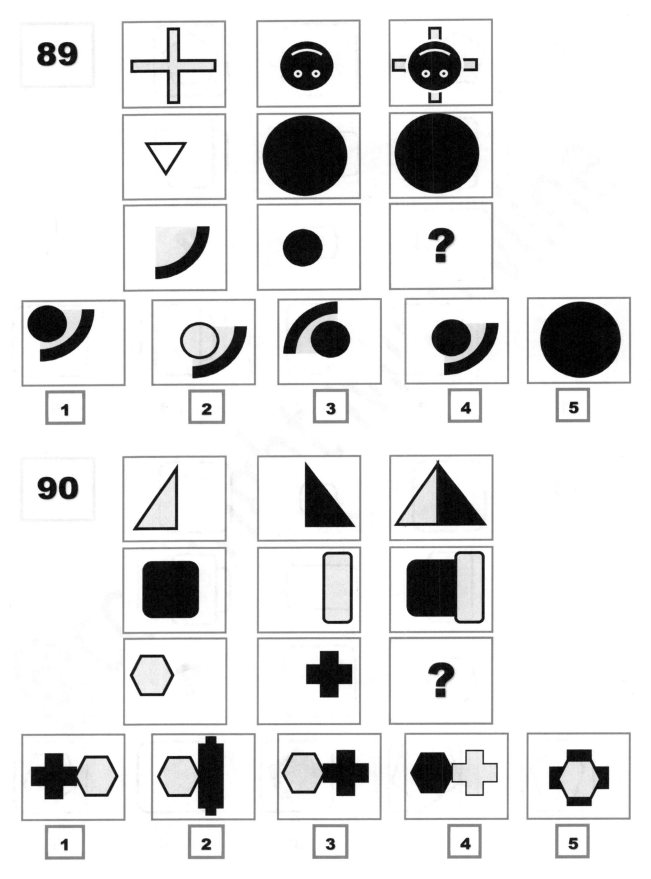

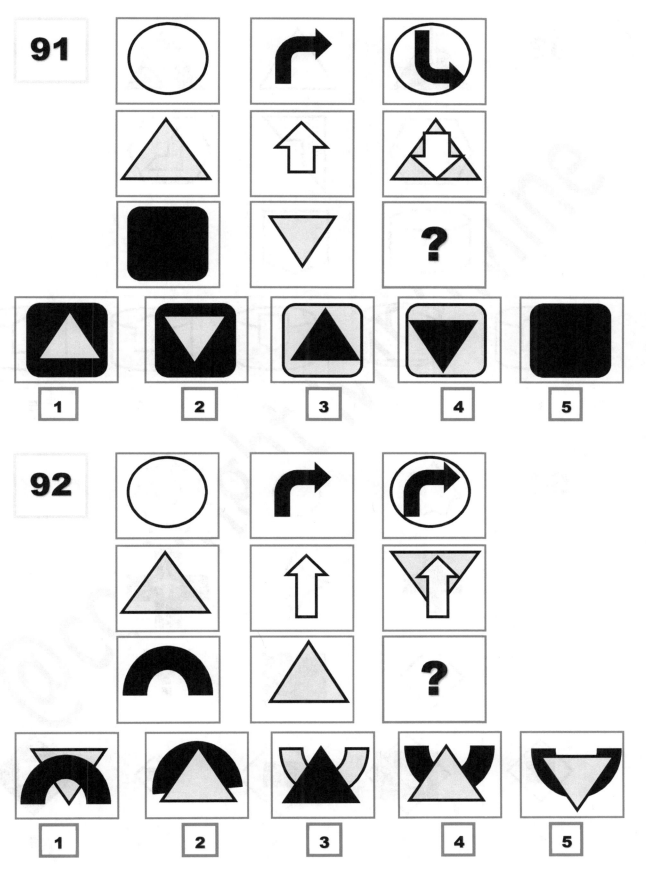

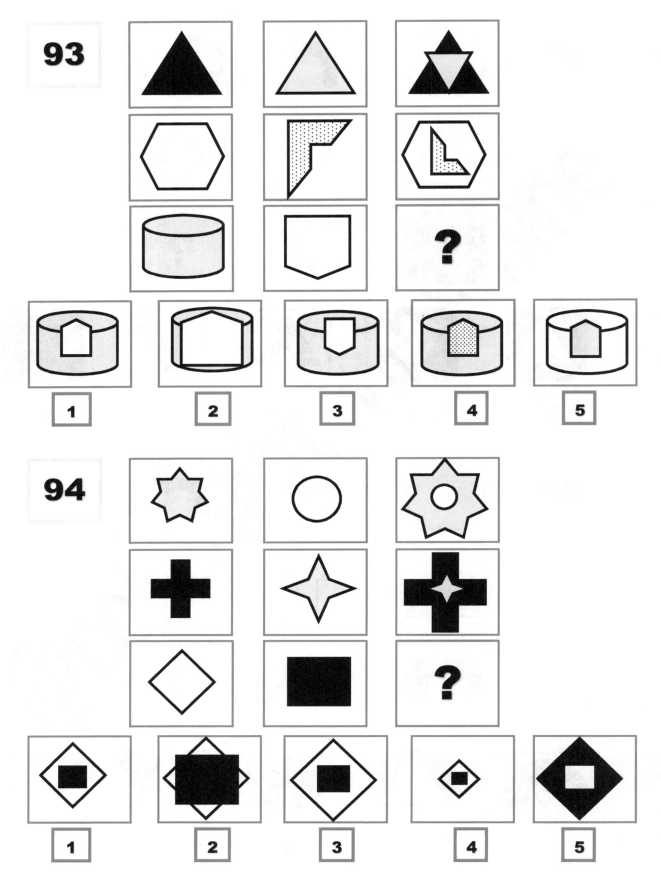

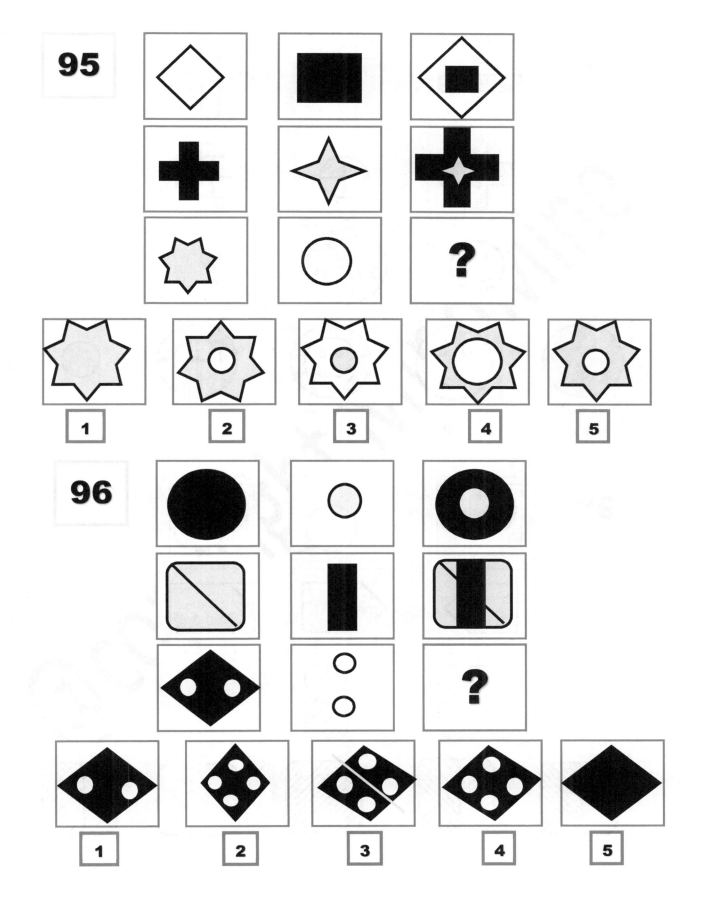

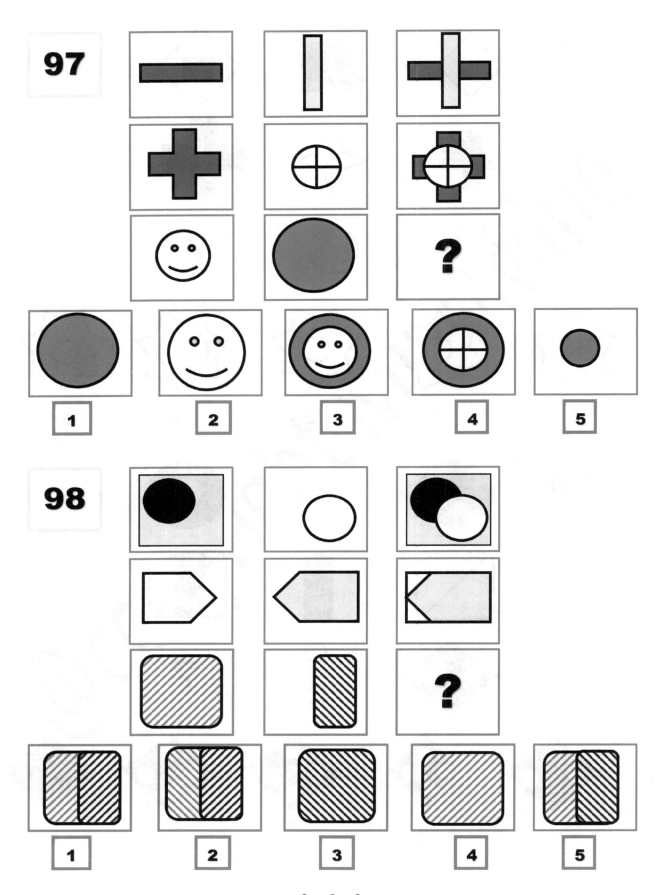

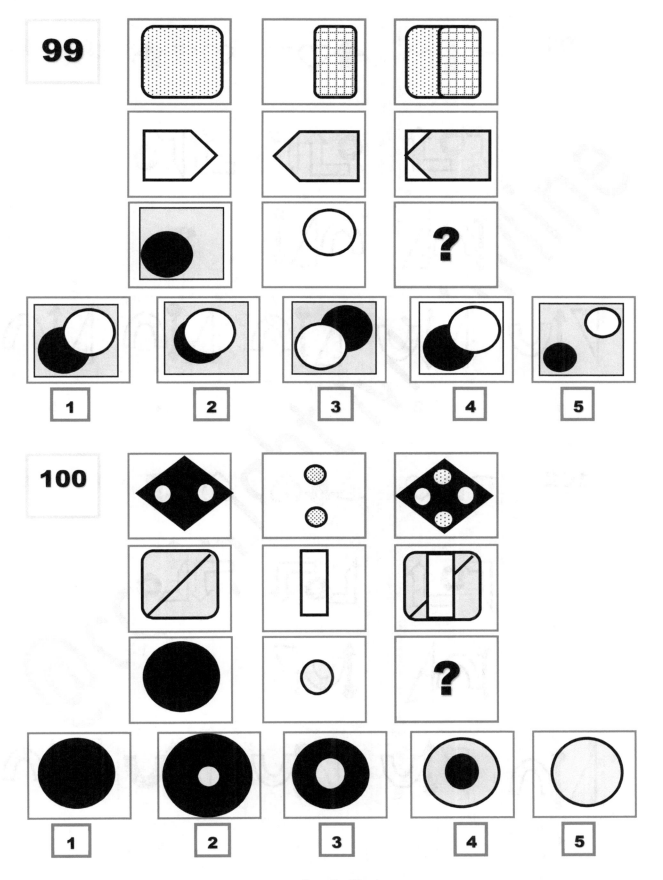

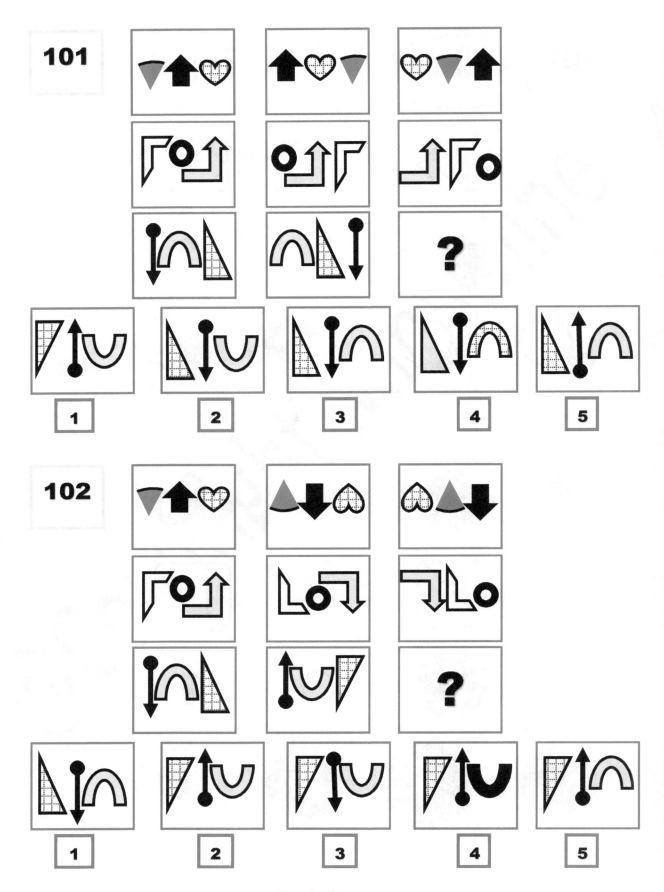

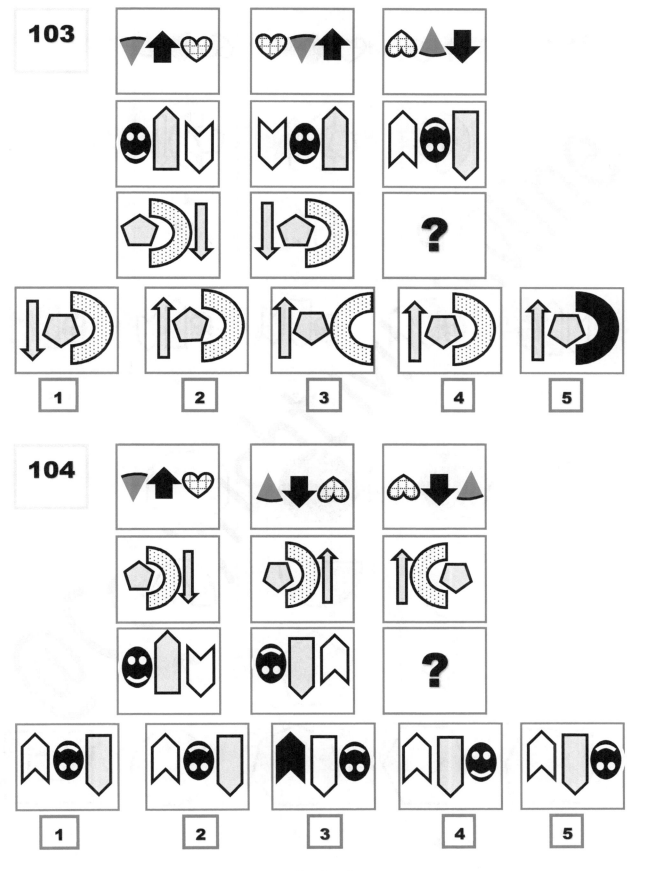

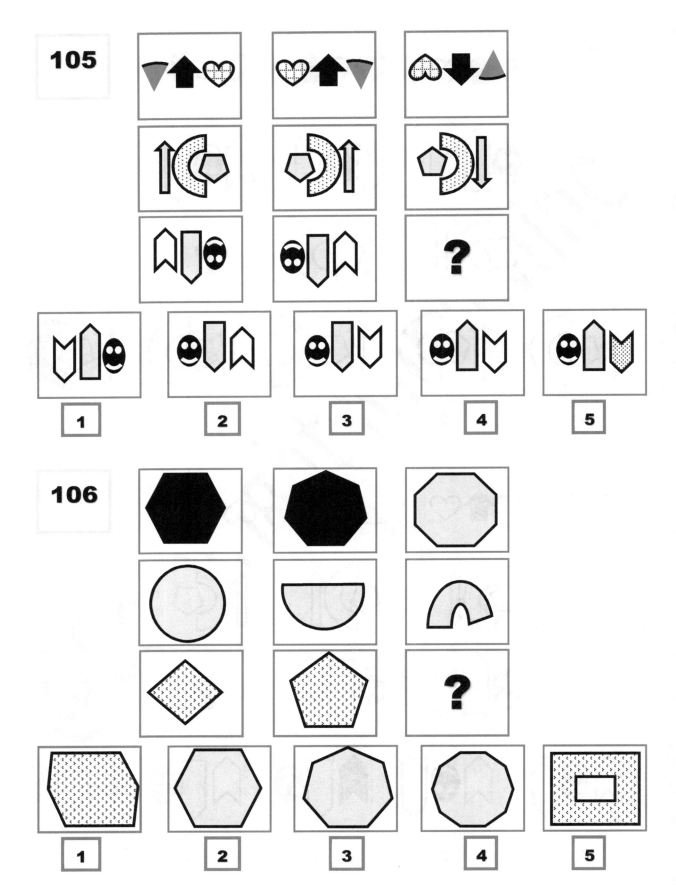

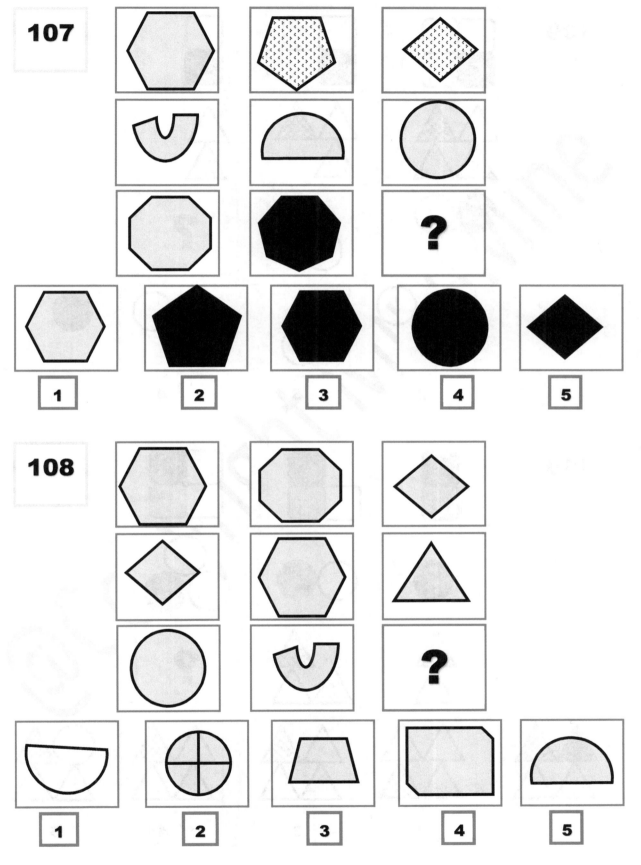

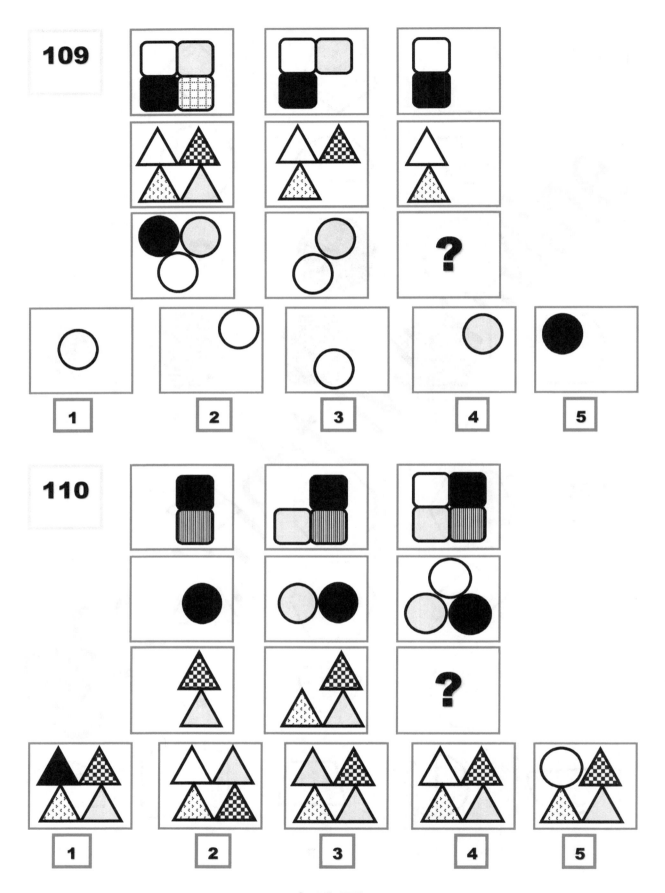

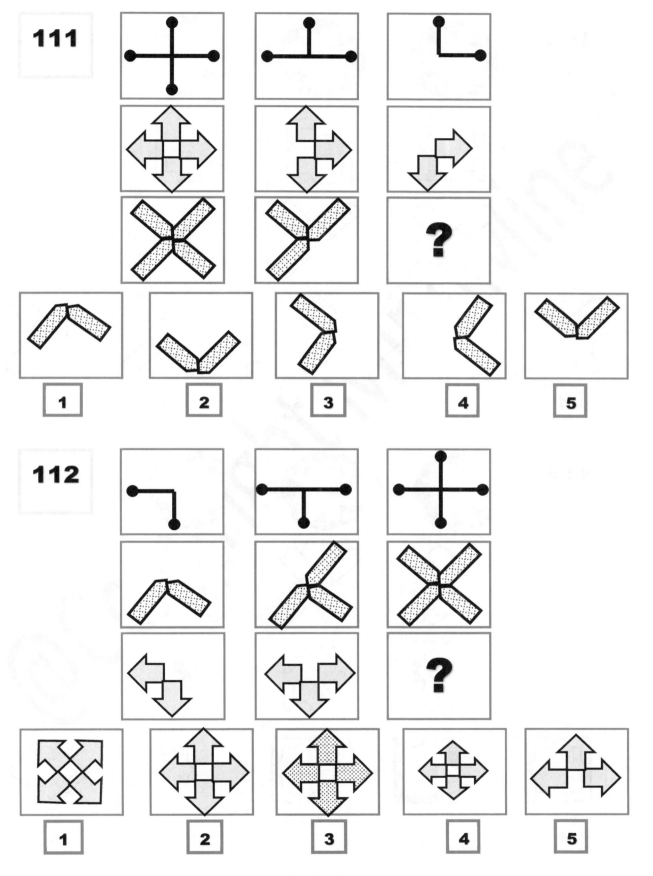

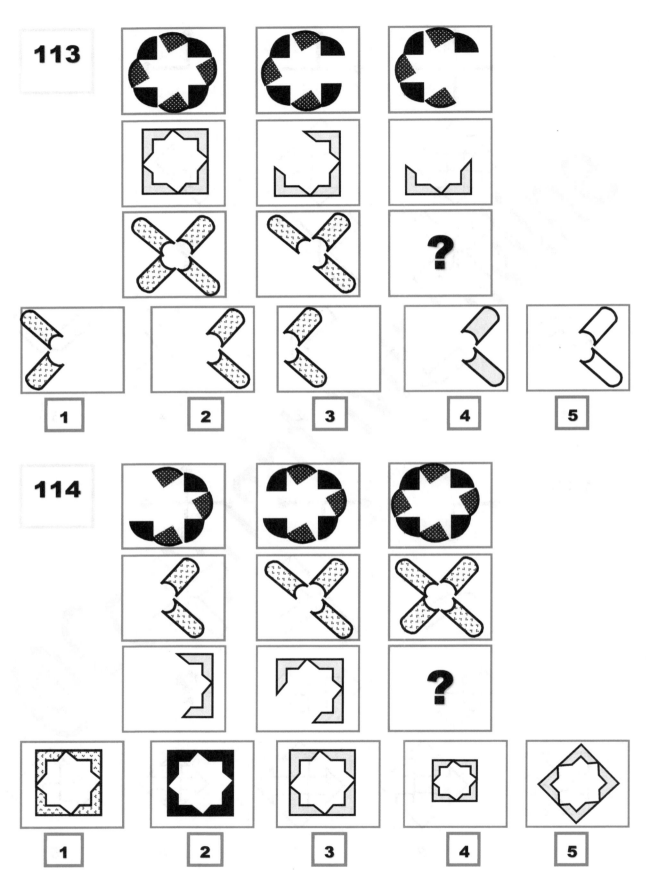

149

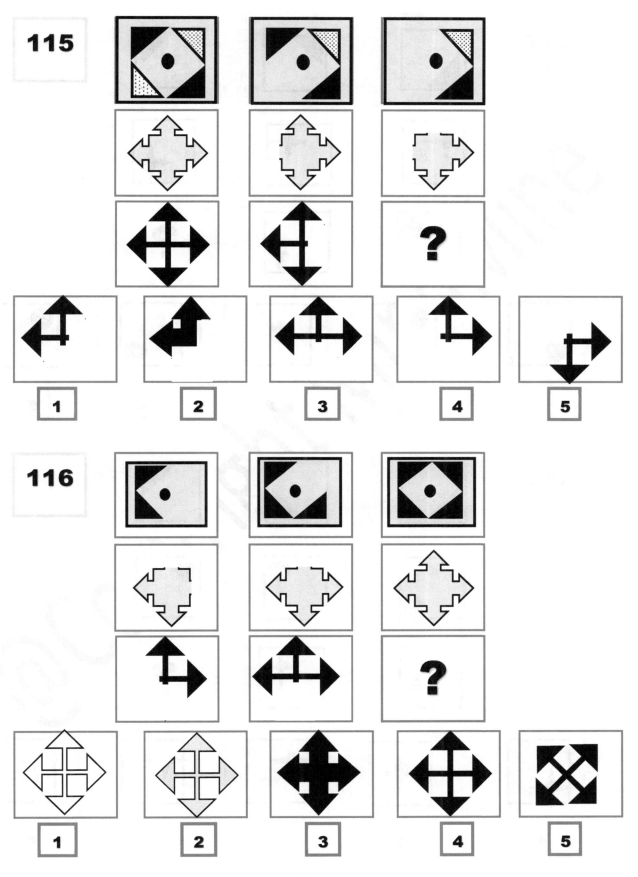

150

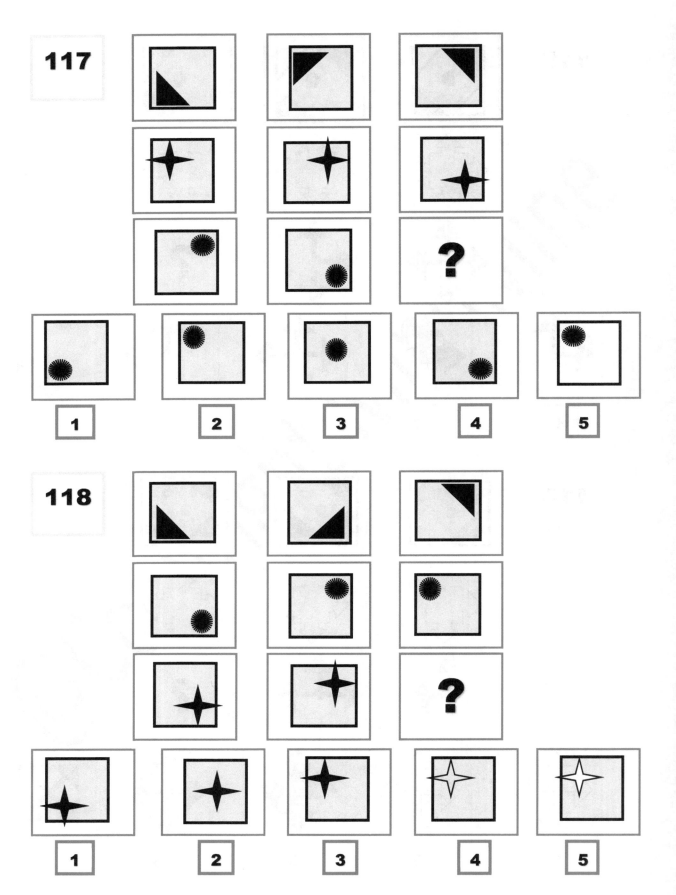

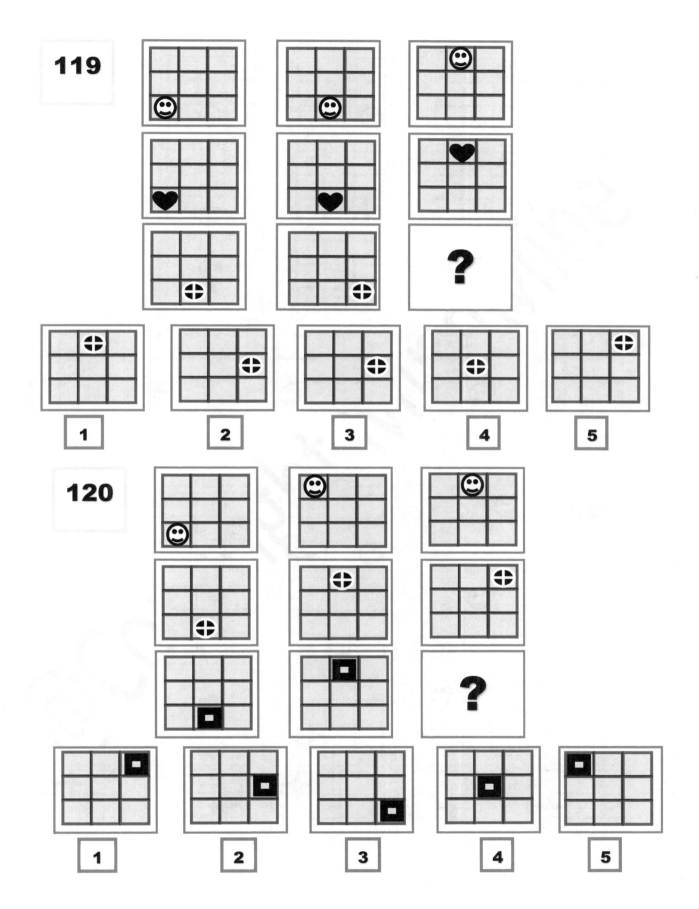

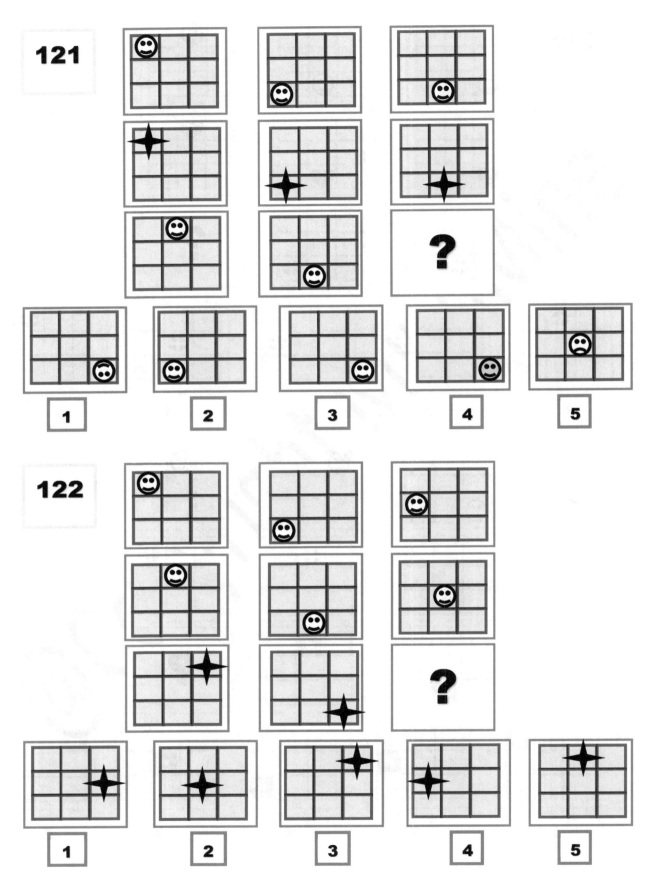

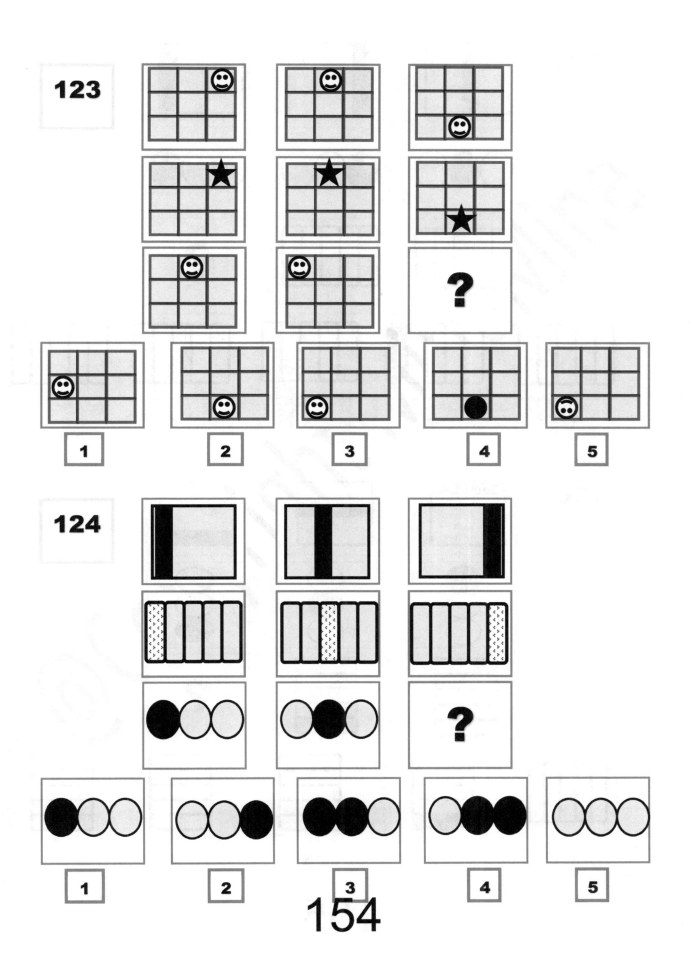

154

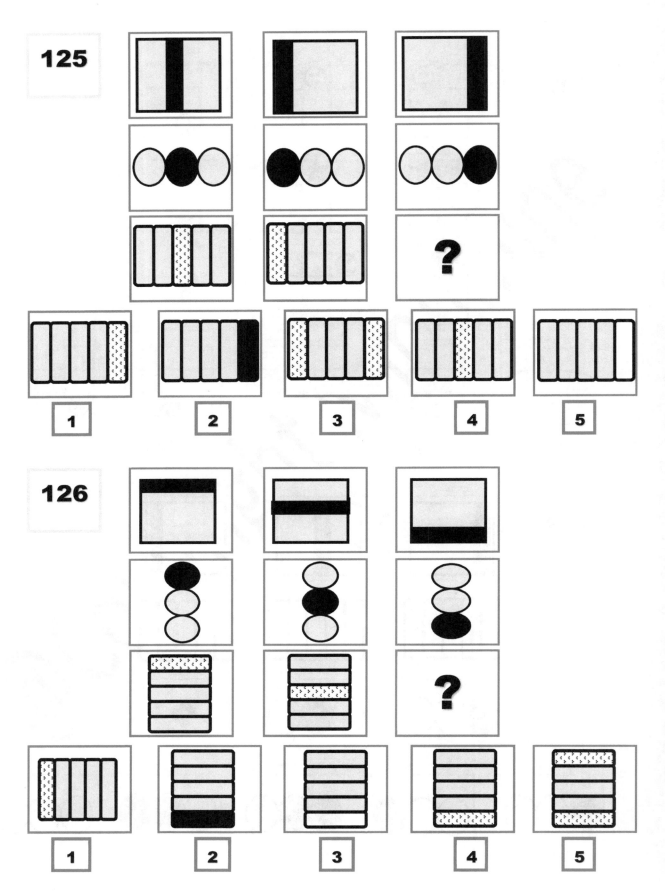

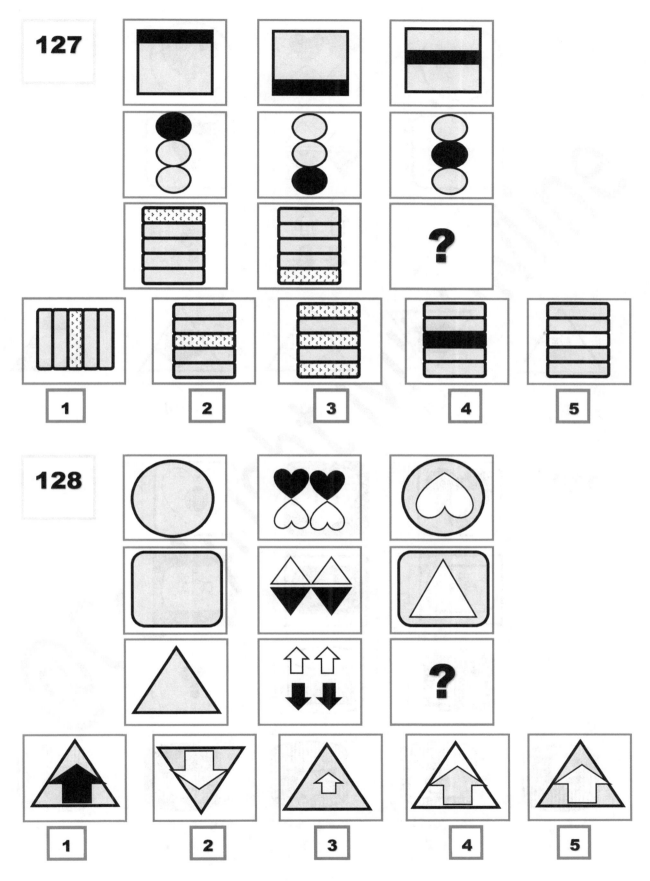

127

128

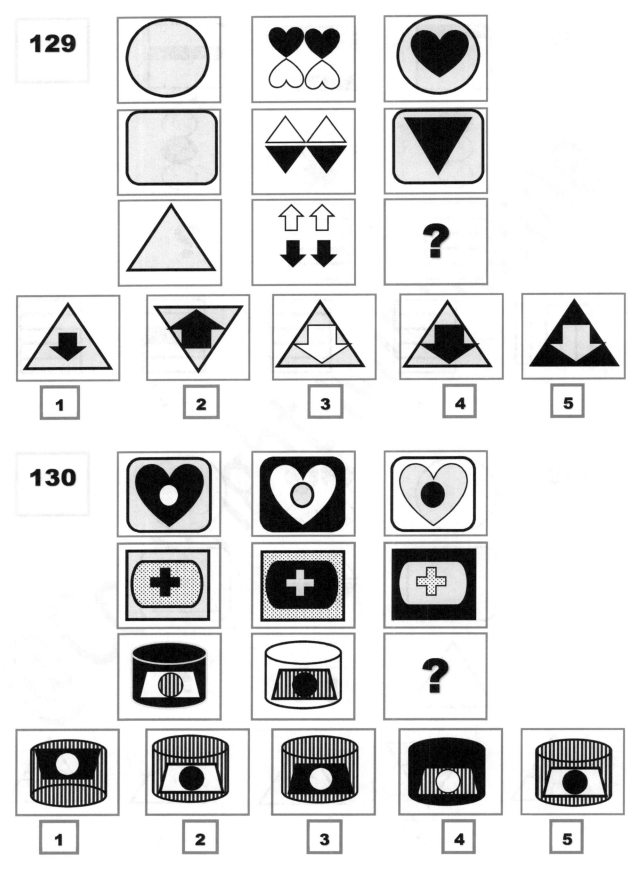

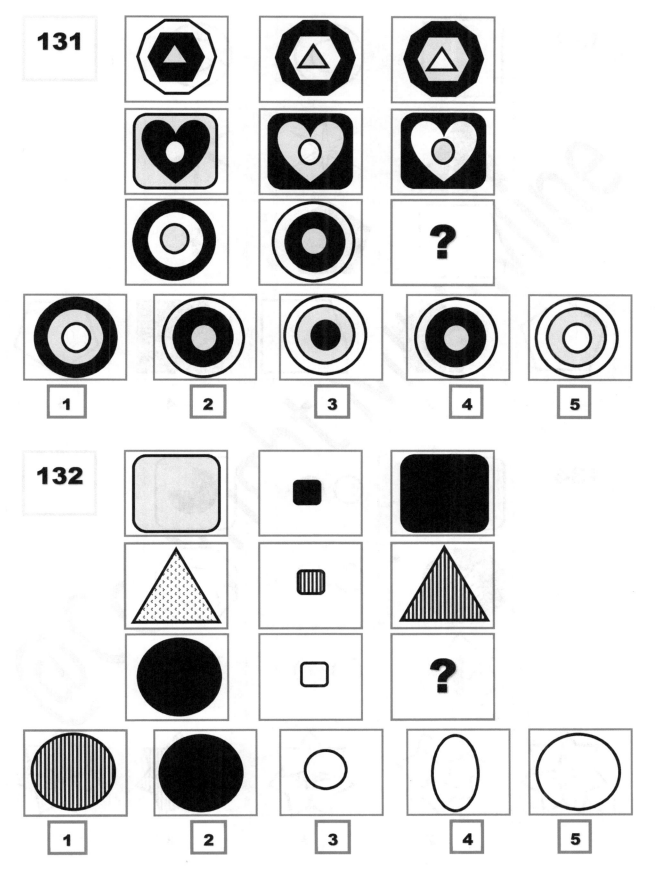

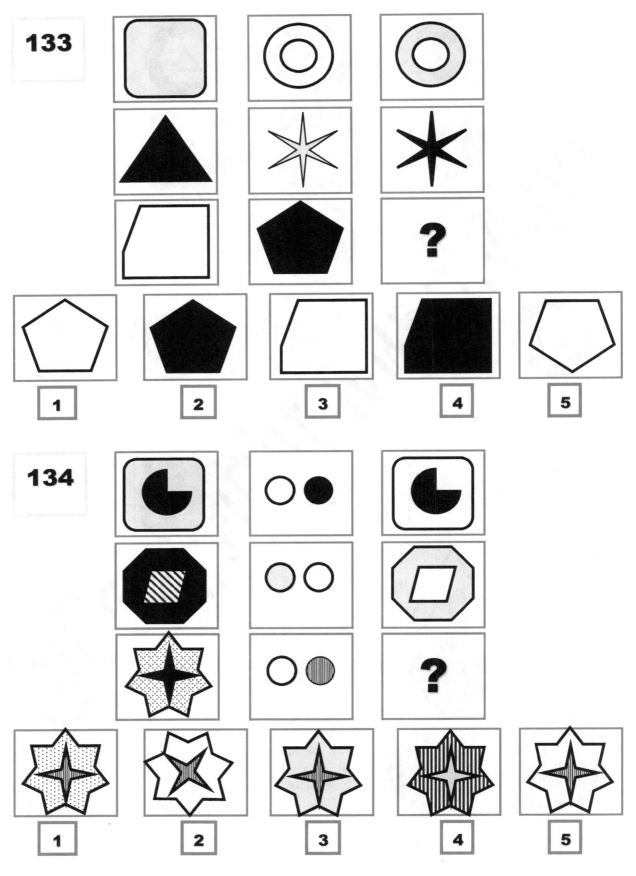

133

134

159

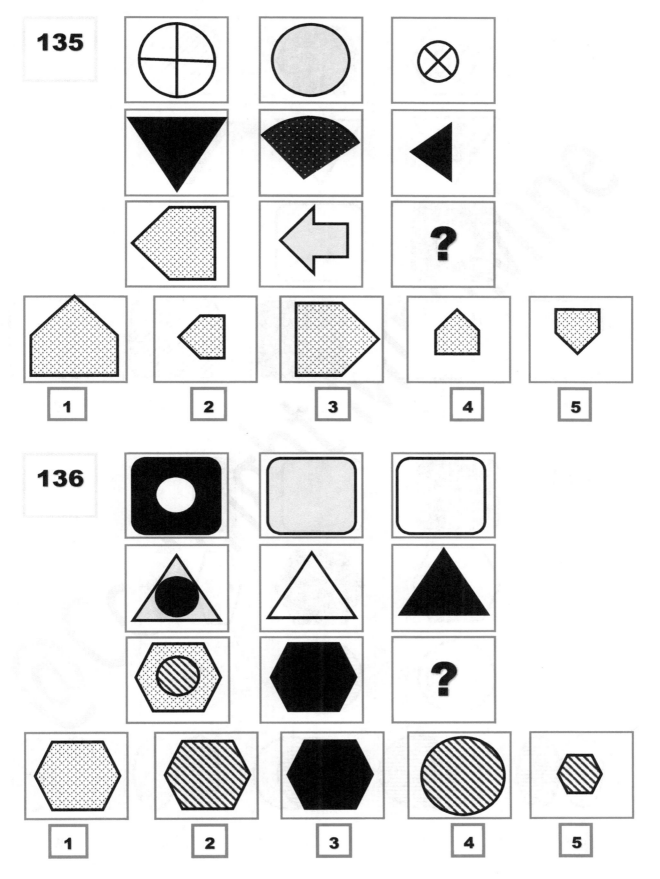

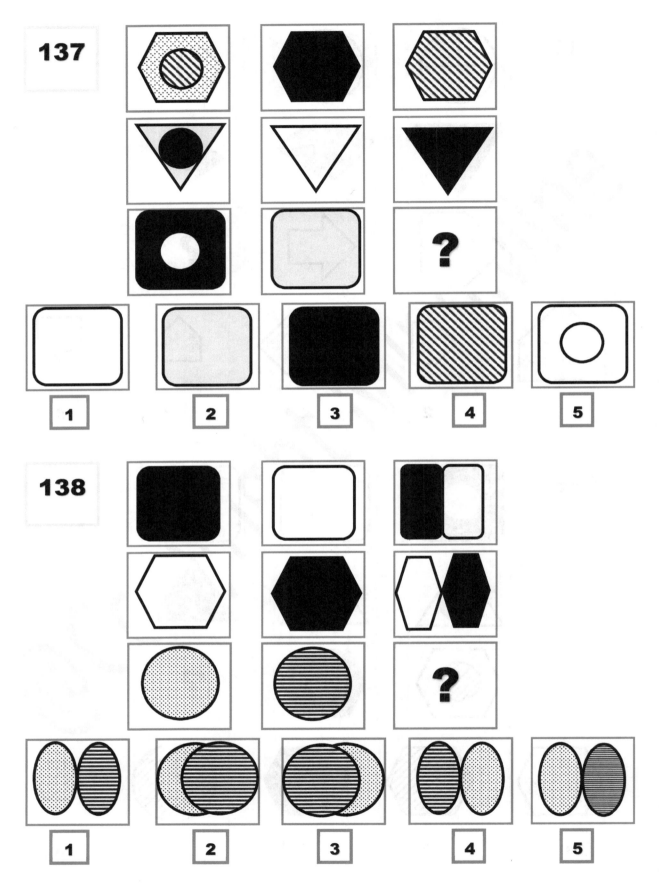

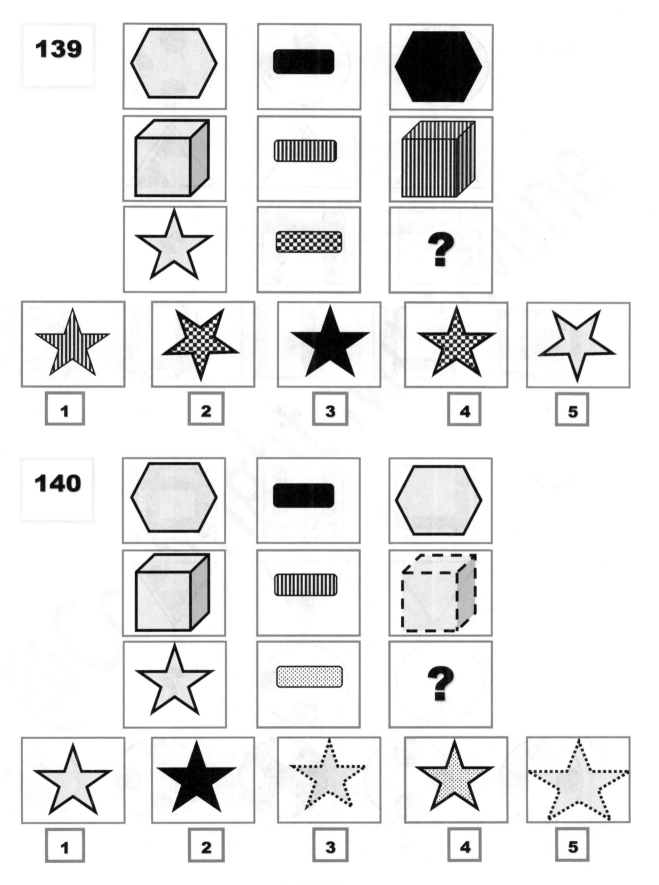

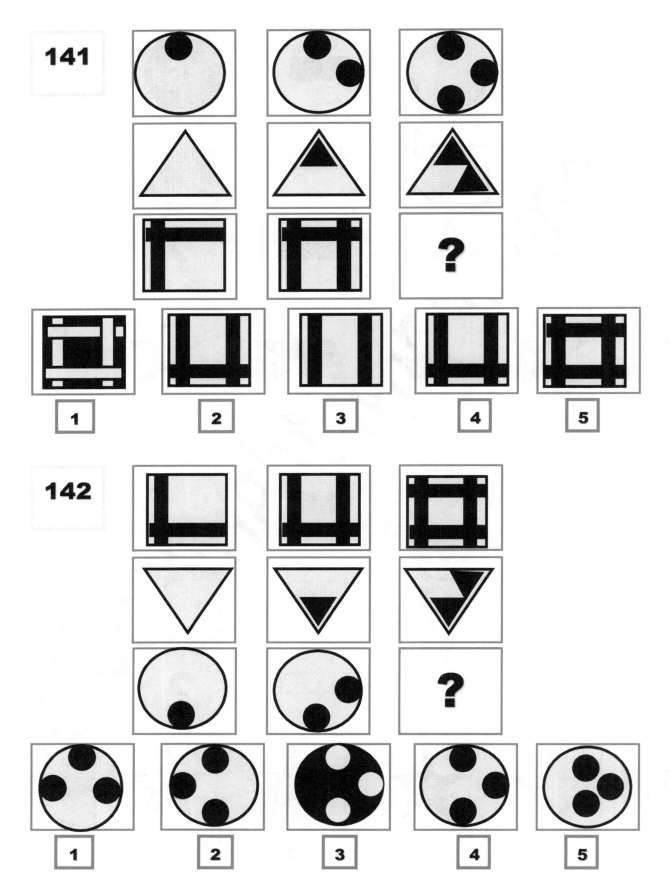

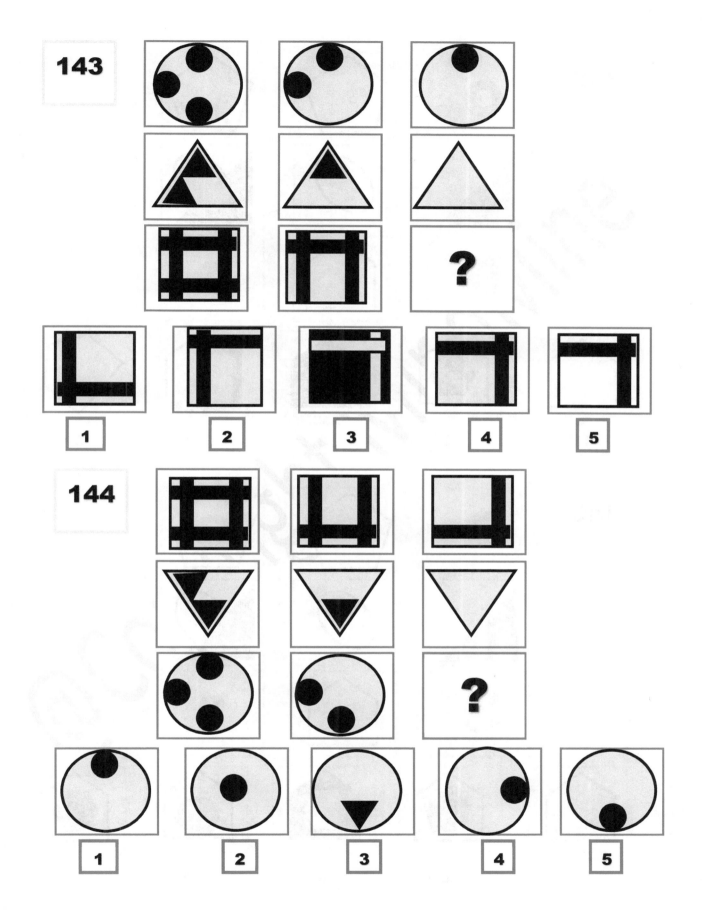

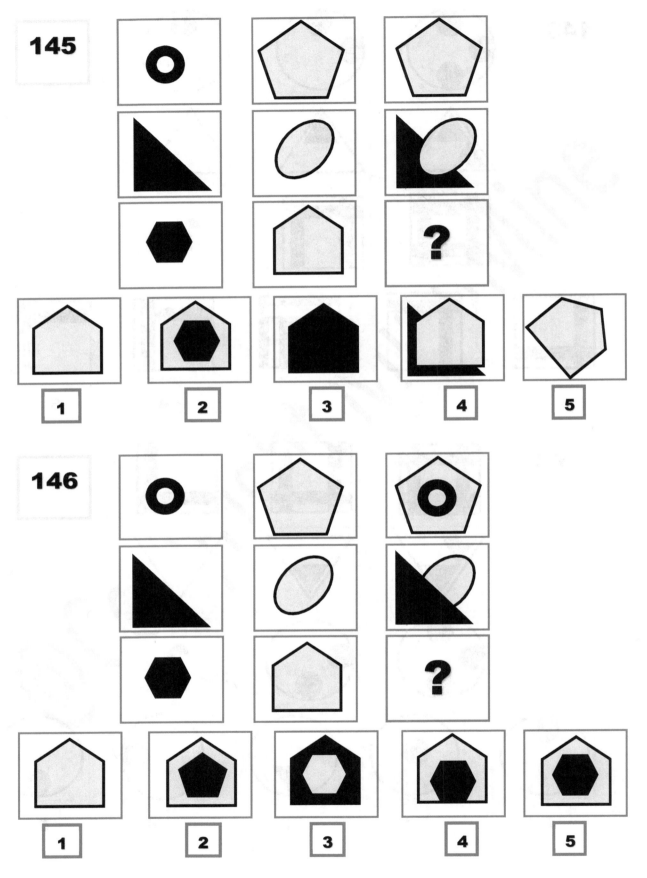

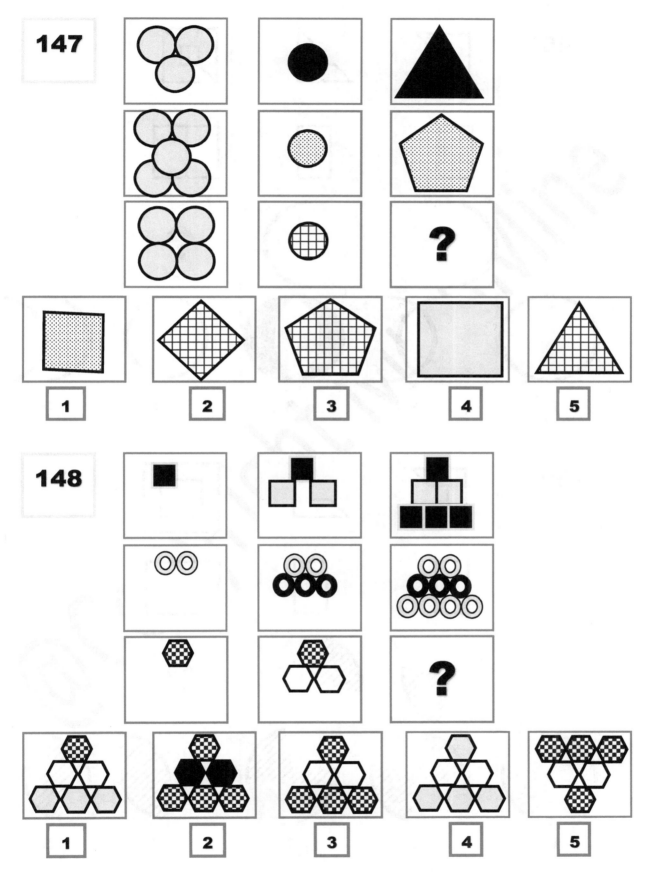

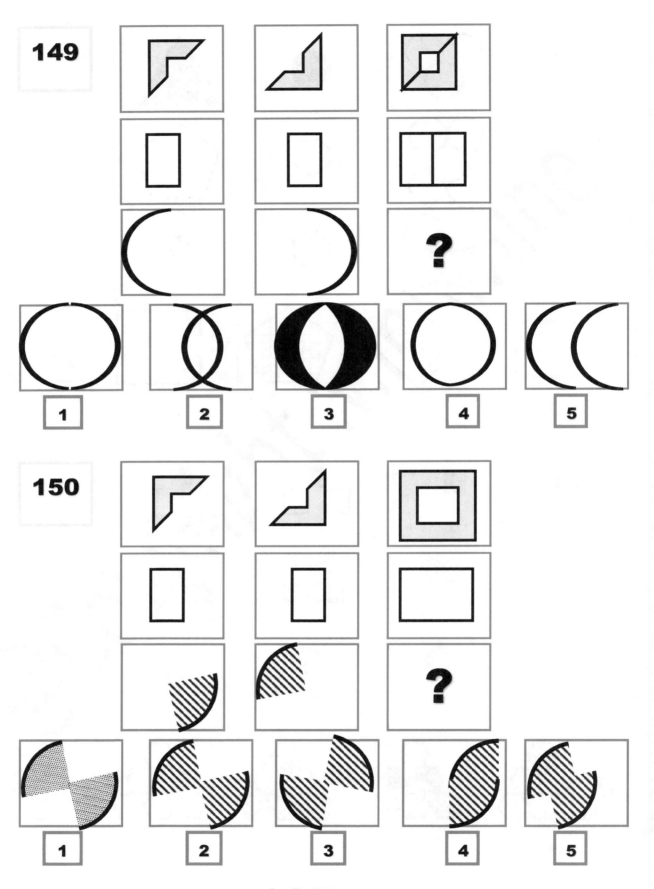

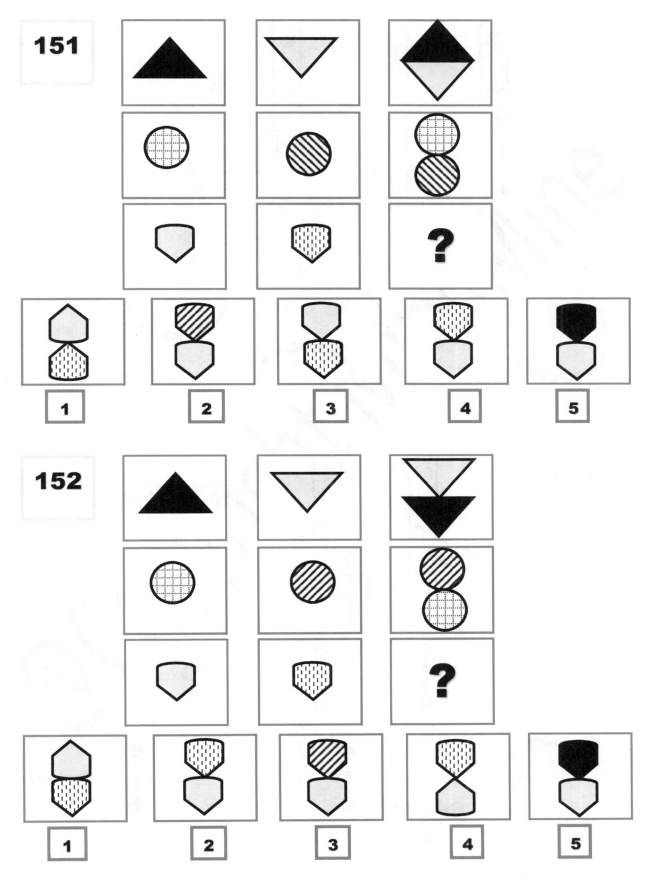

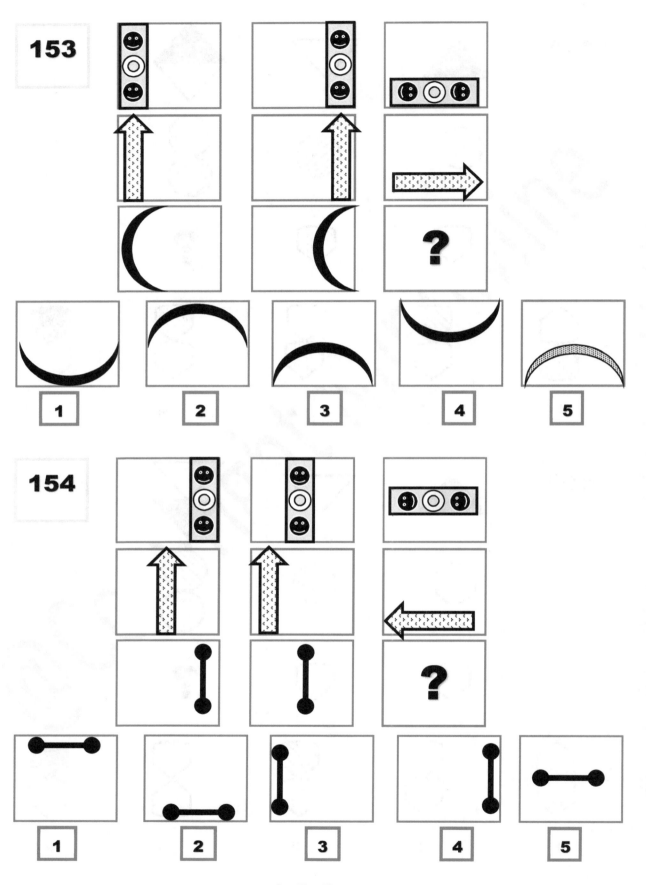

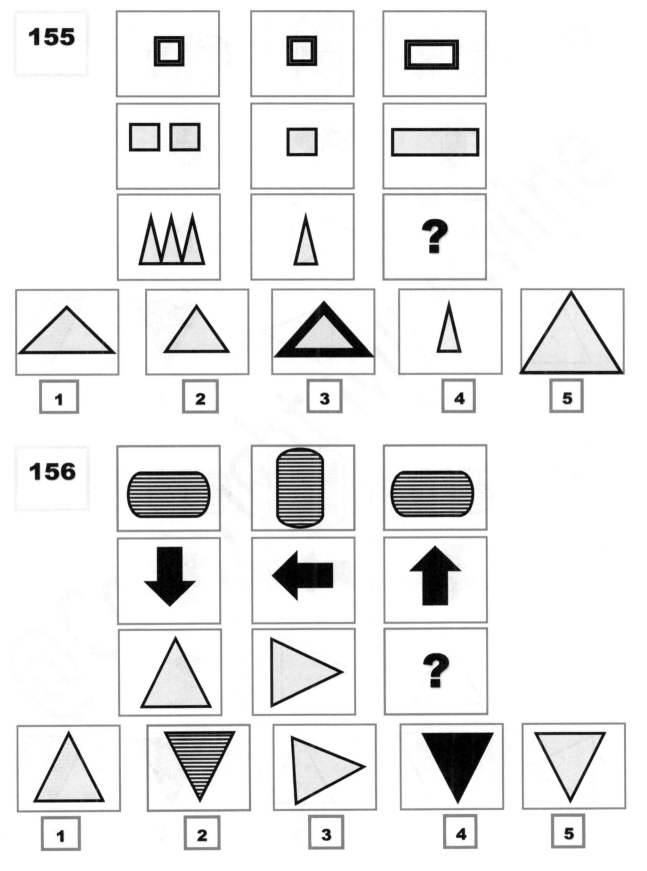

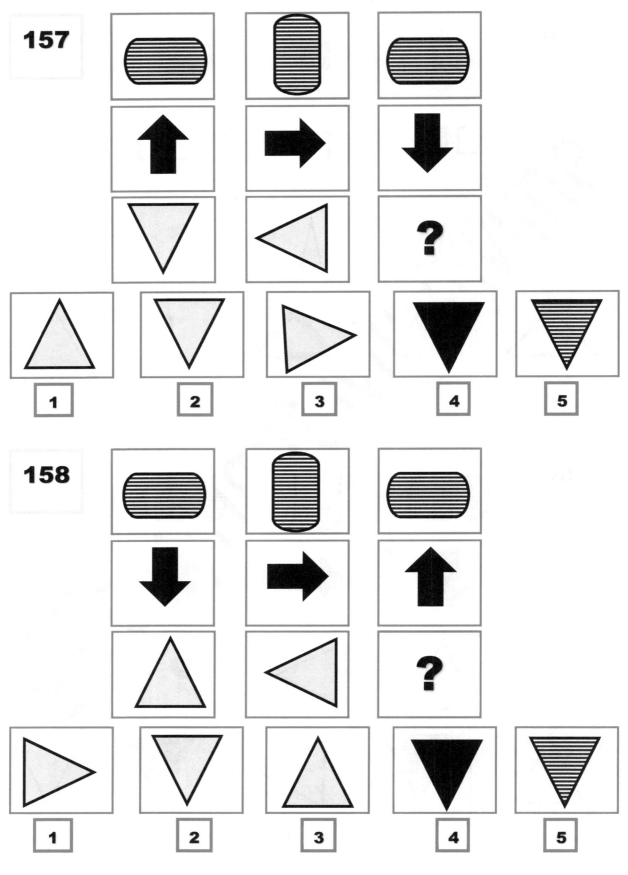

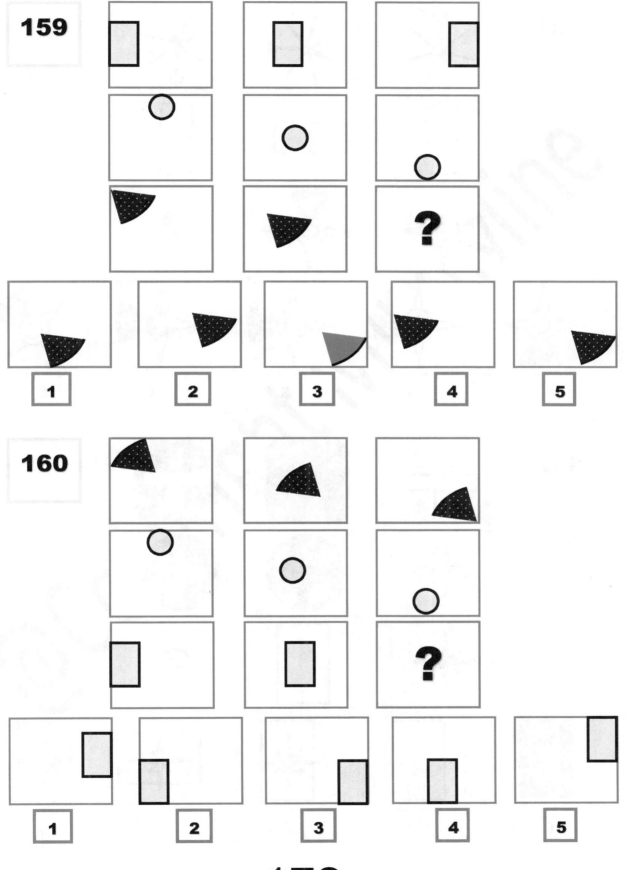

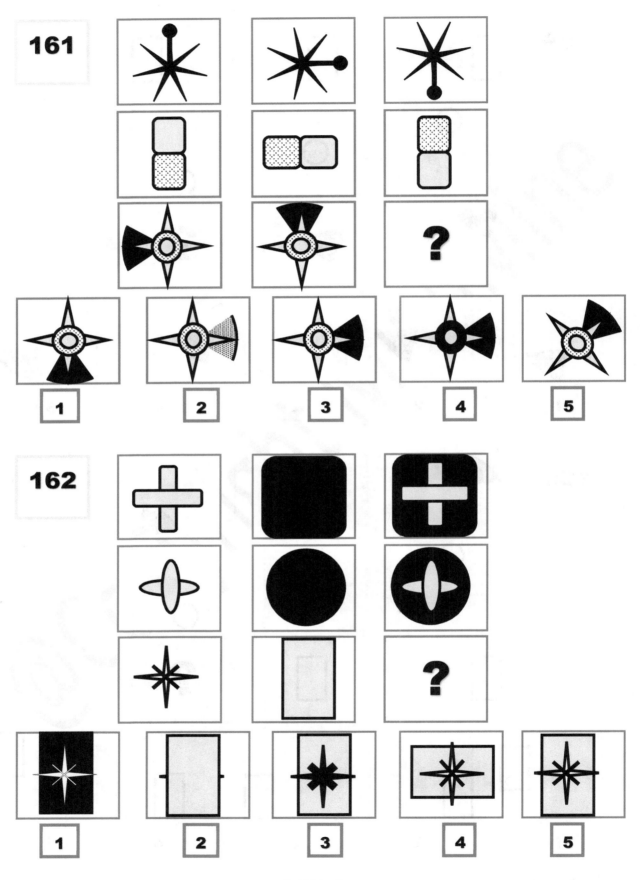

173

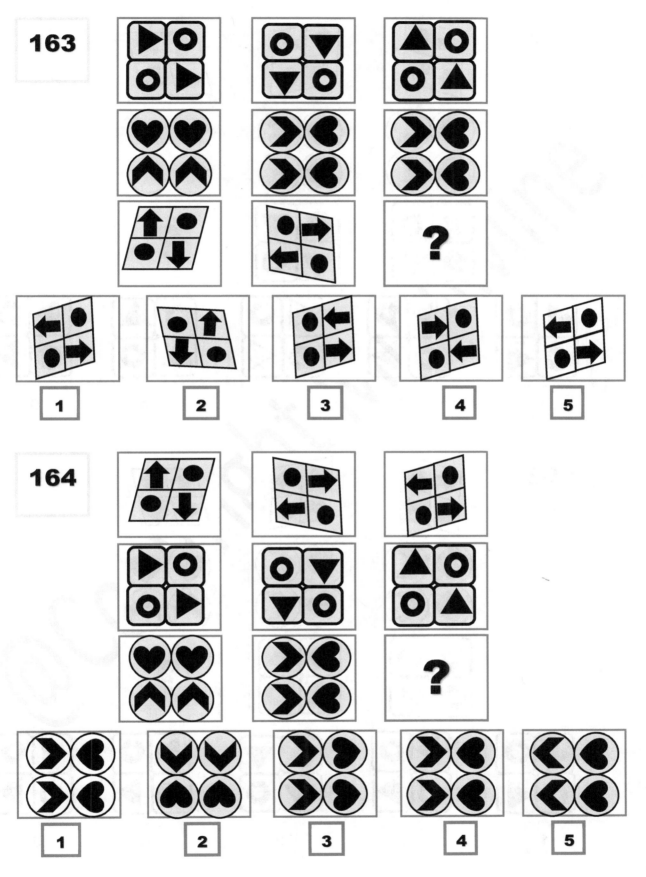

163

164

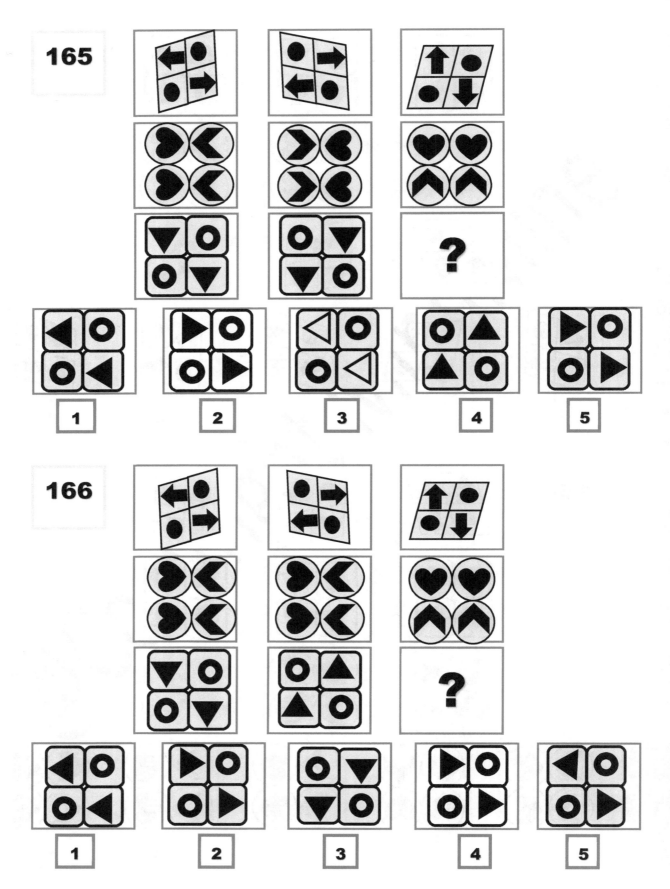

175

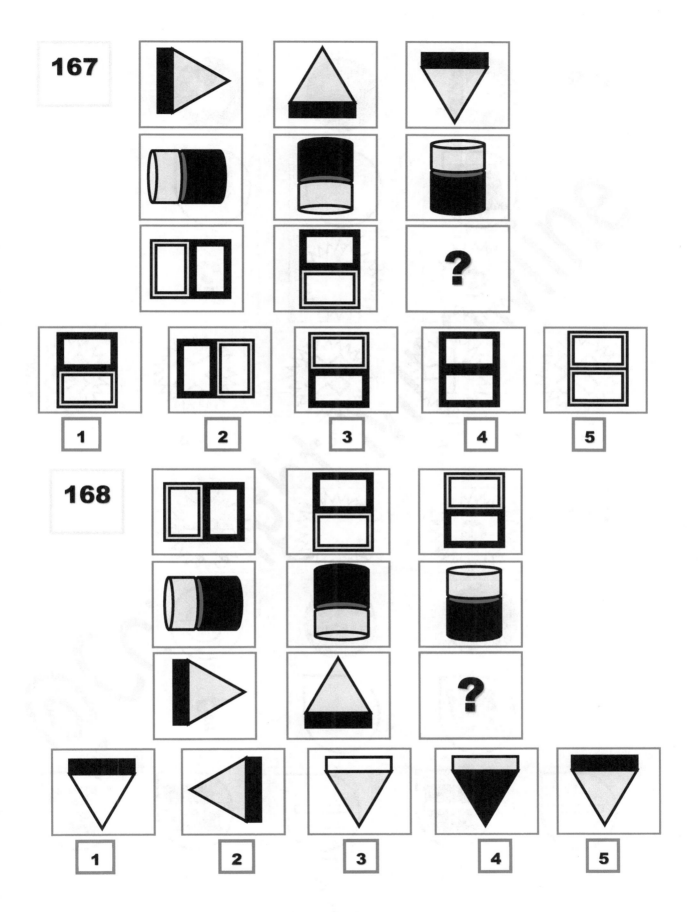

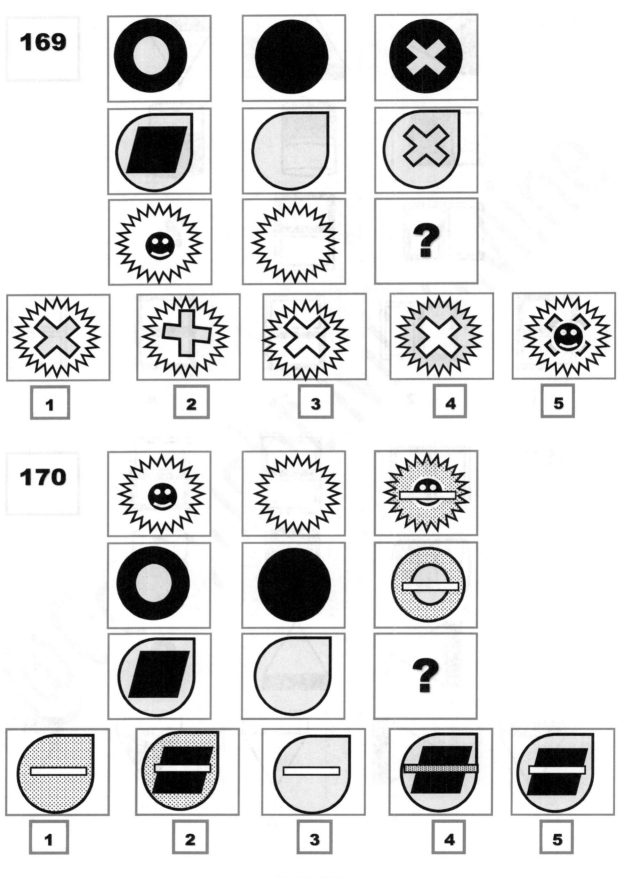

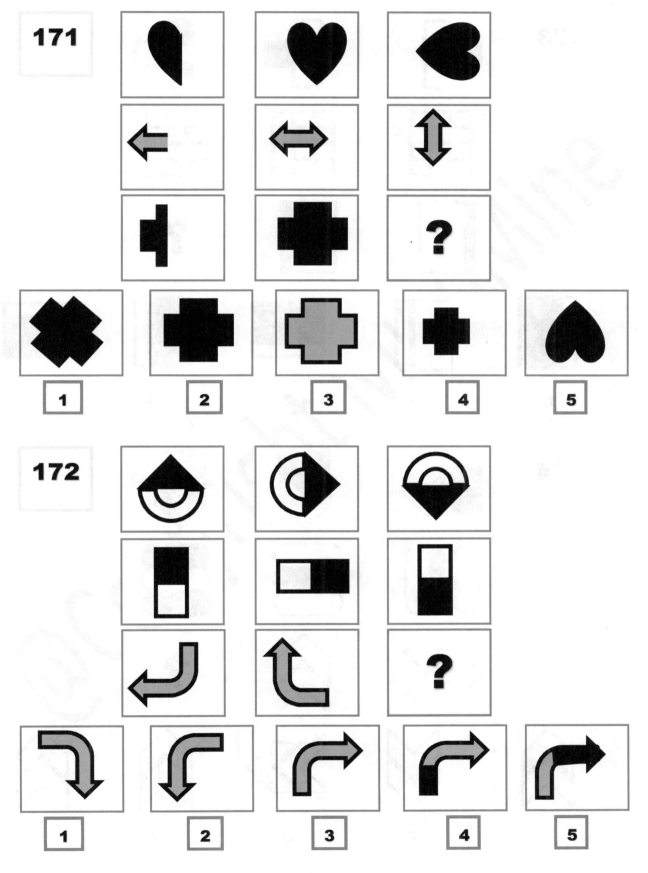

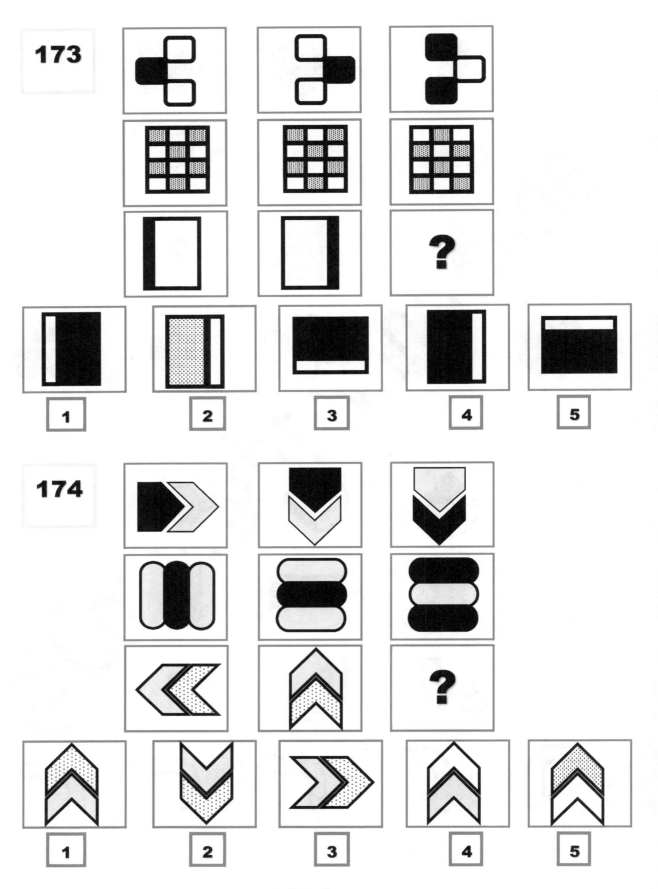

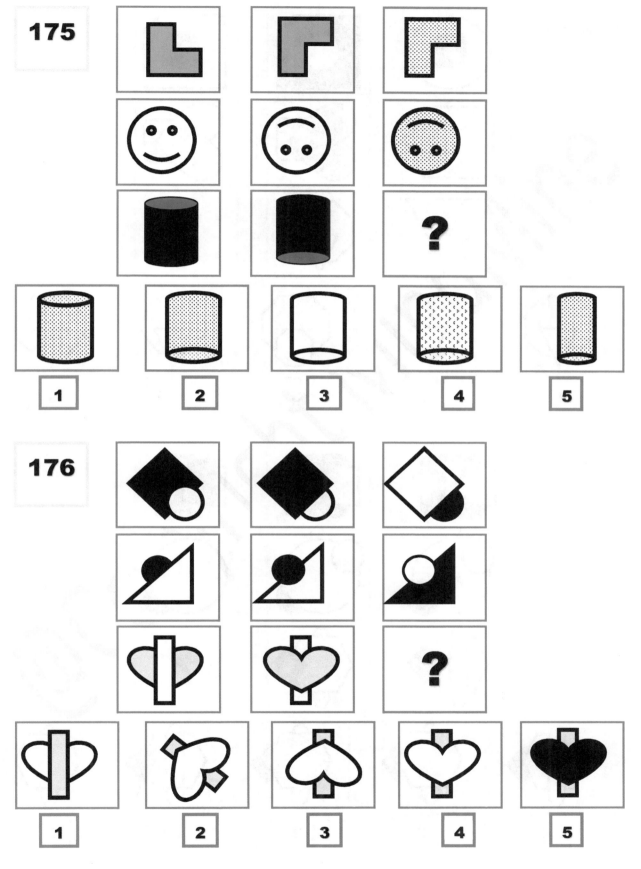

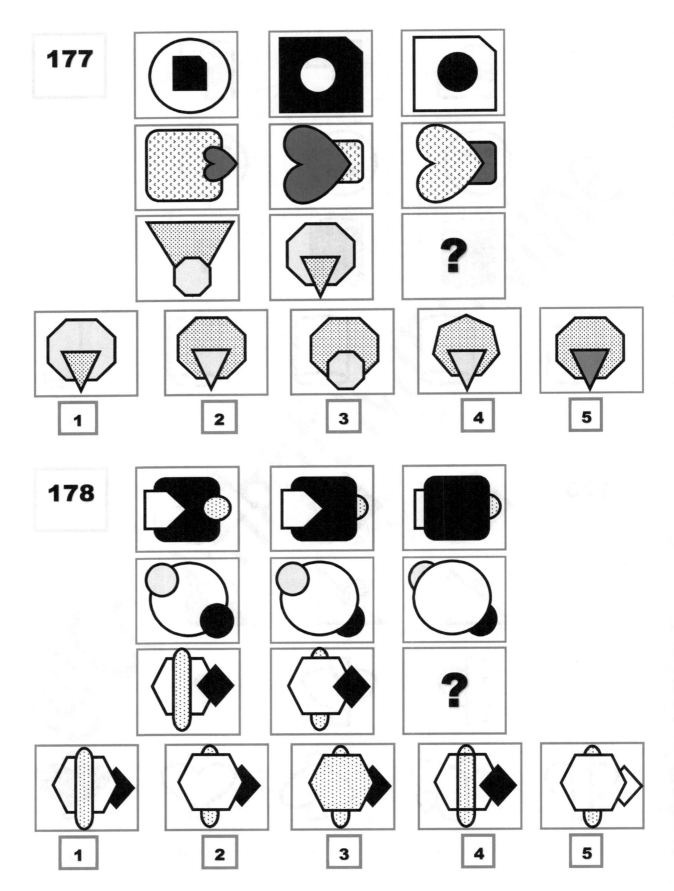

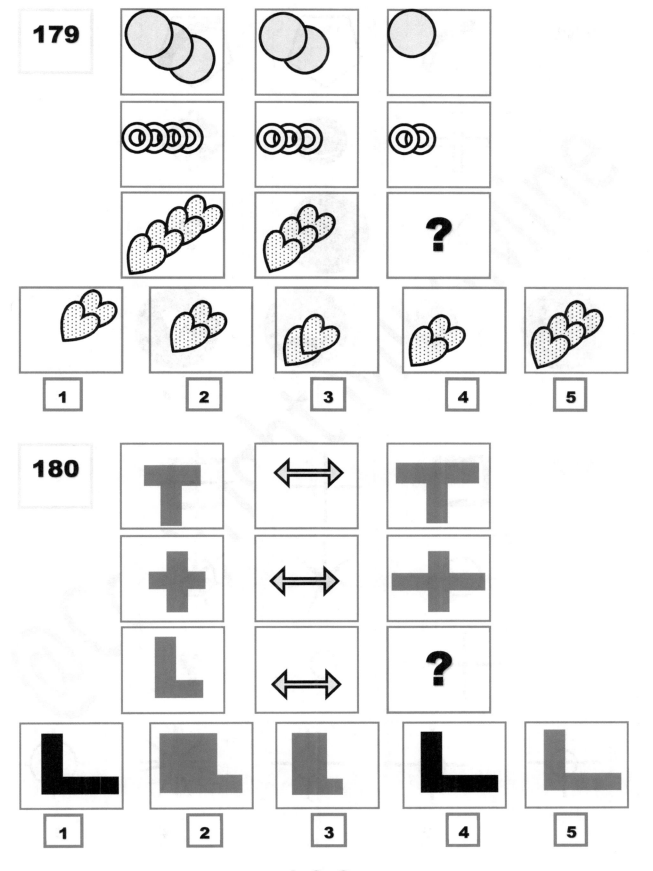

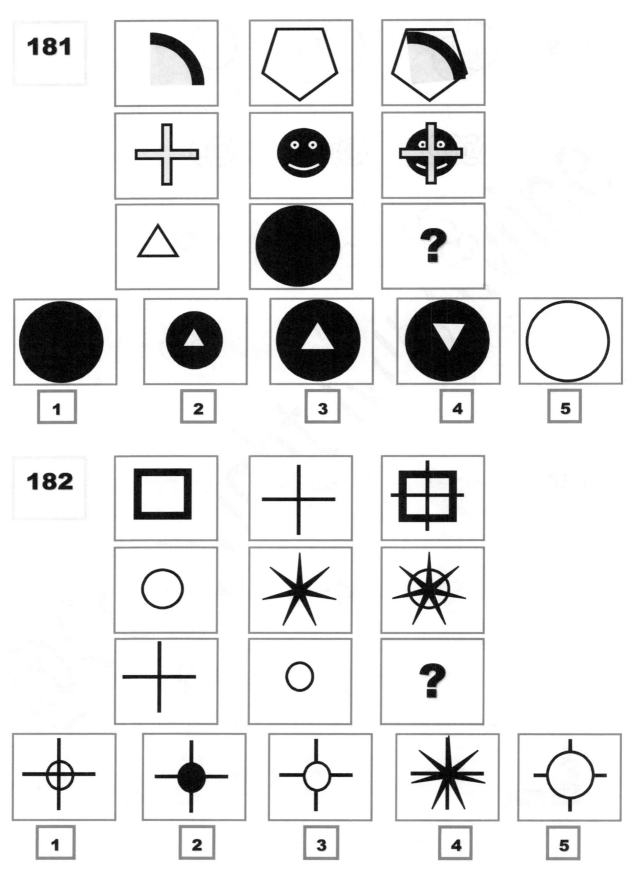

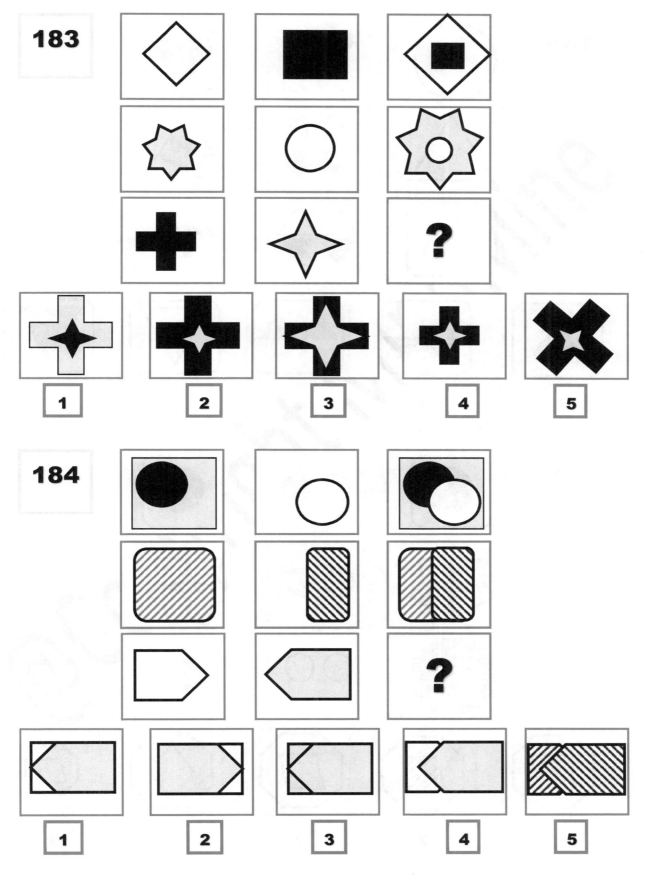

183

184

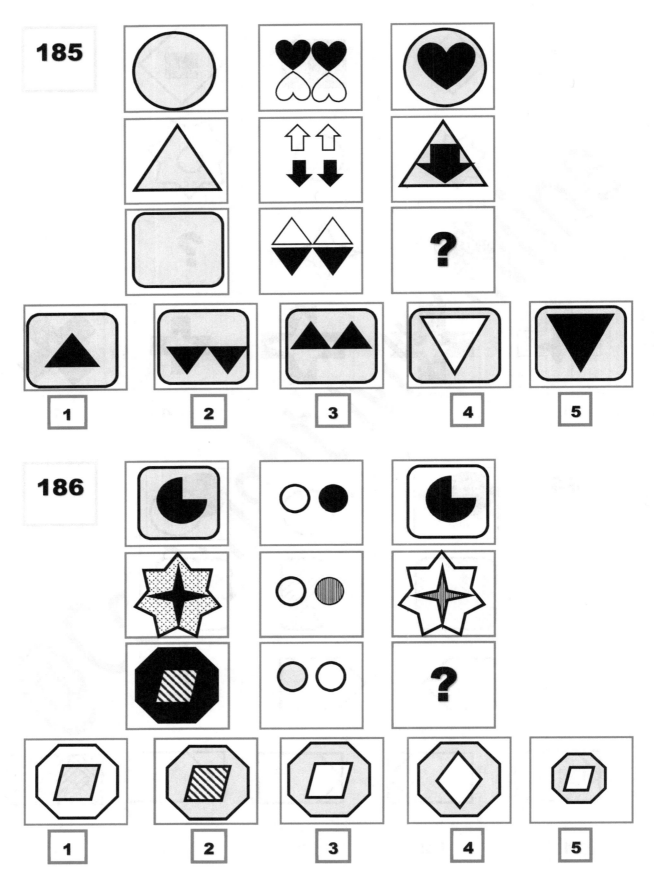

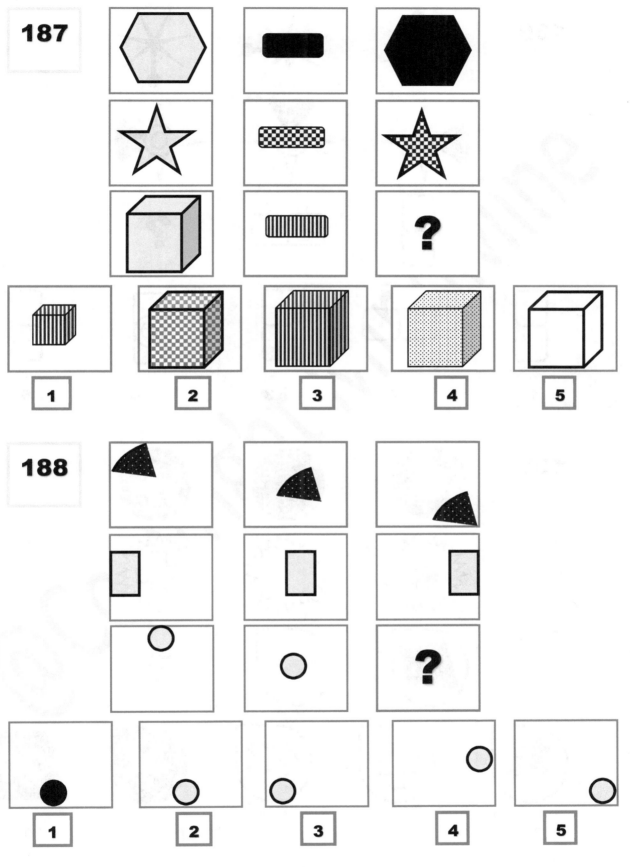

187

188

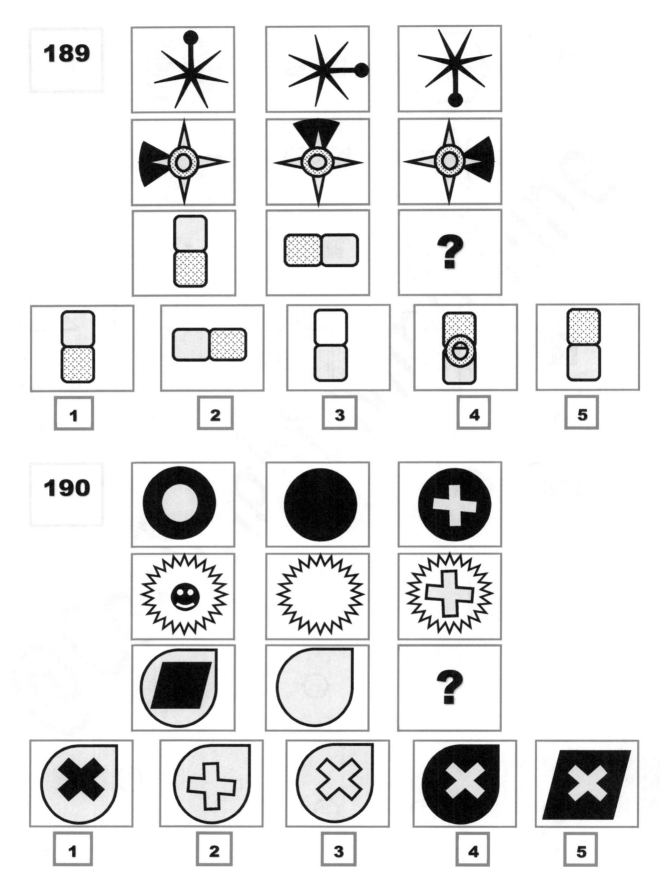

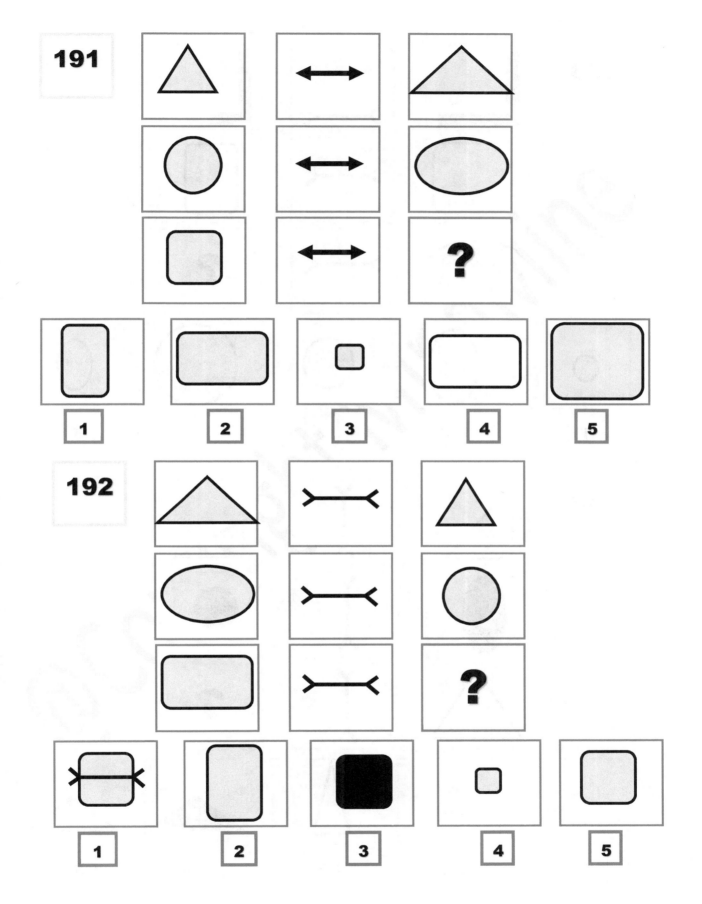

191

192

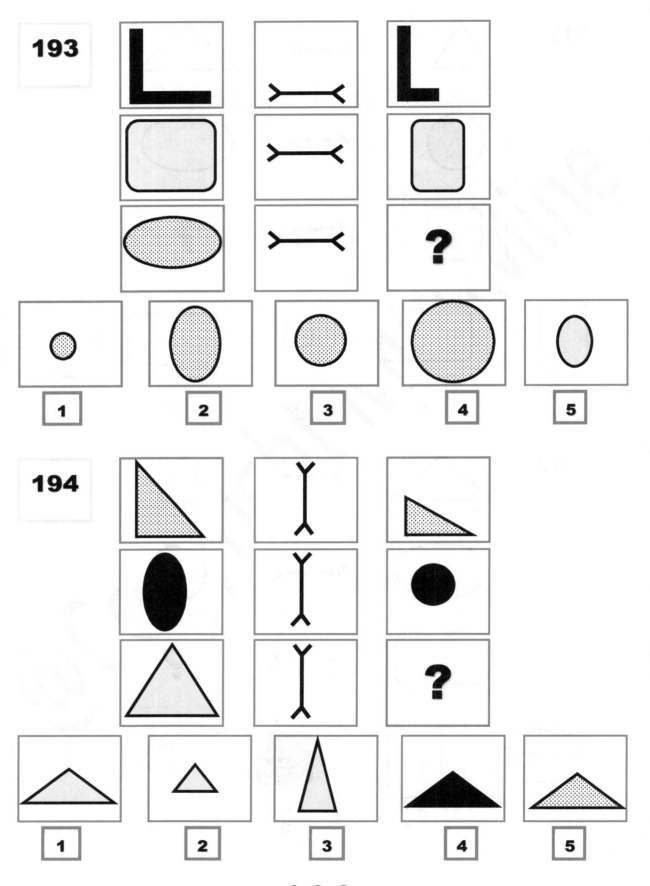

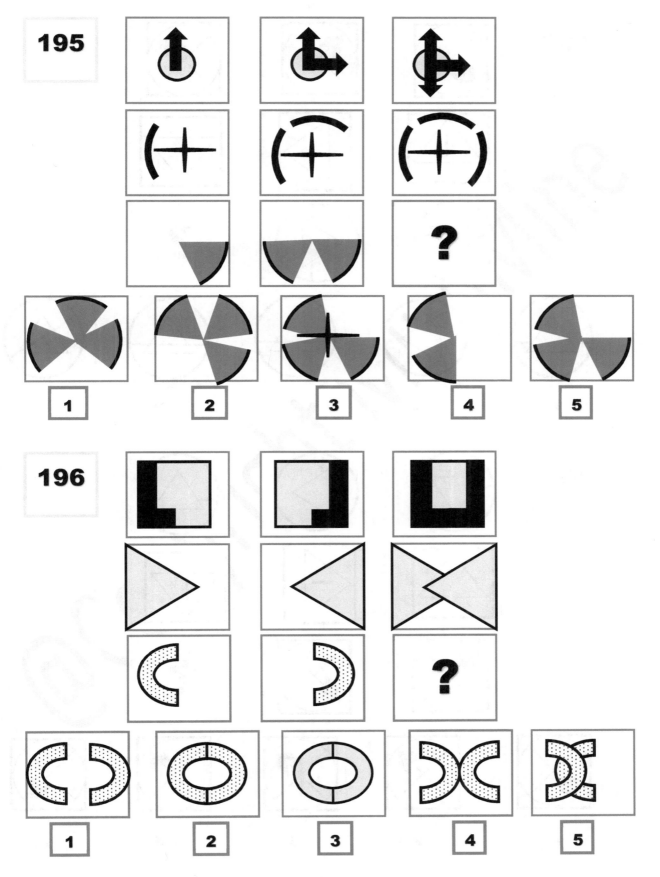

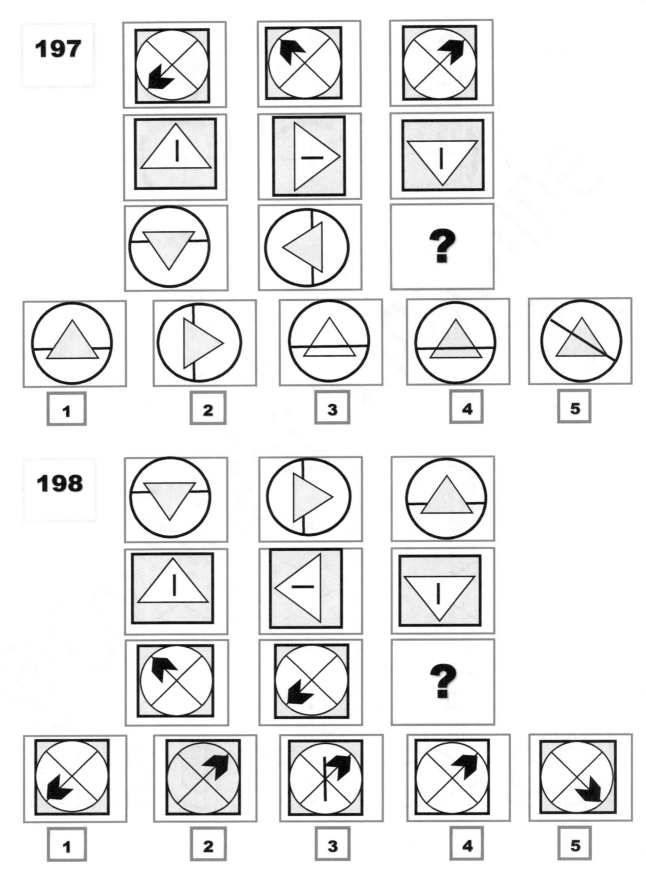

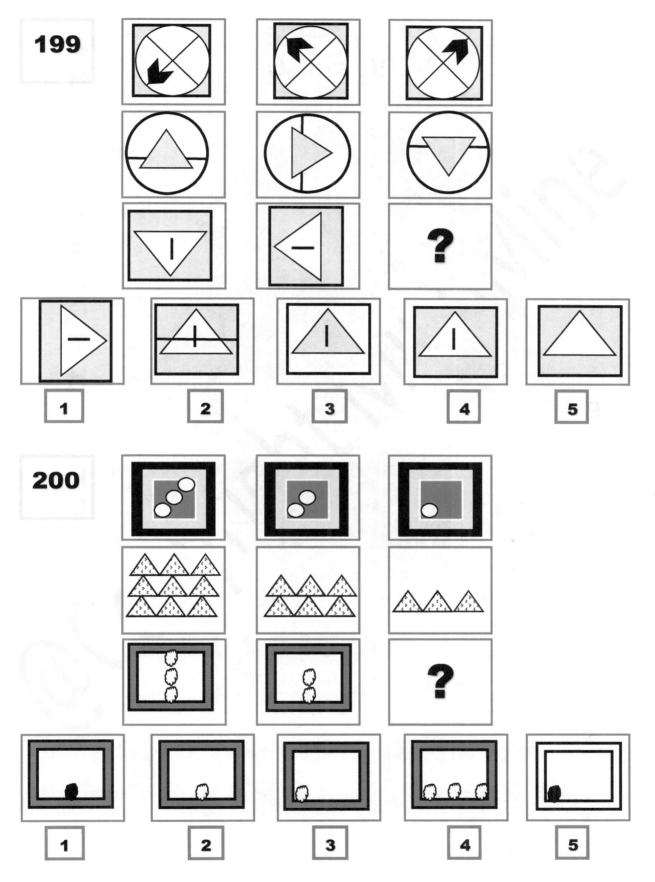

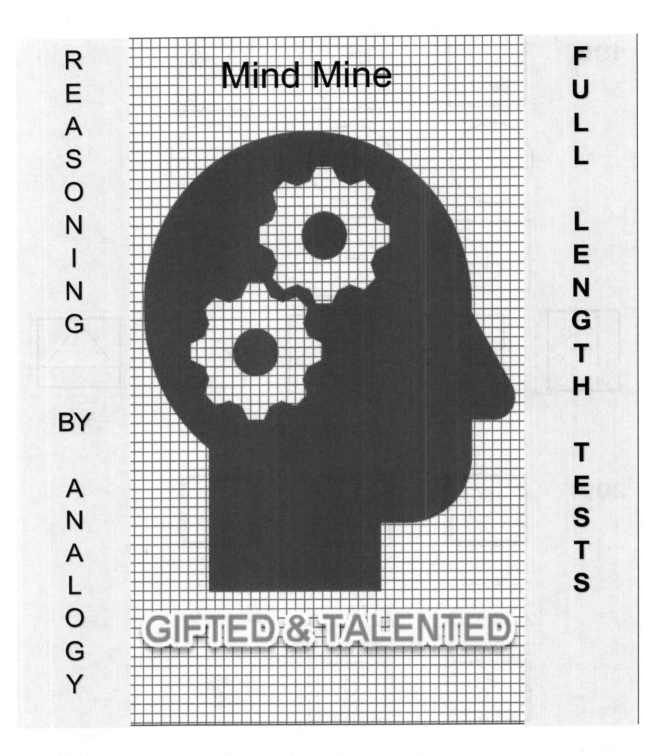

REASONING BY ANALOGY

FULL LENGTH TESTS

GIFTED & TALENTED

PRACTICE
TEST #1

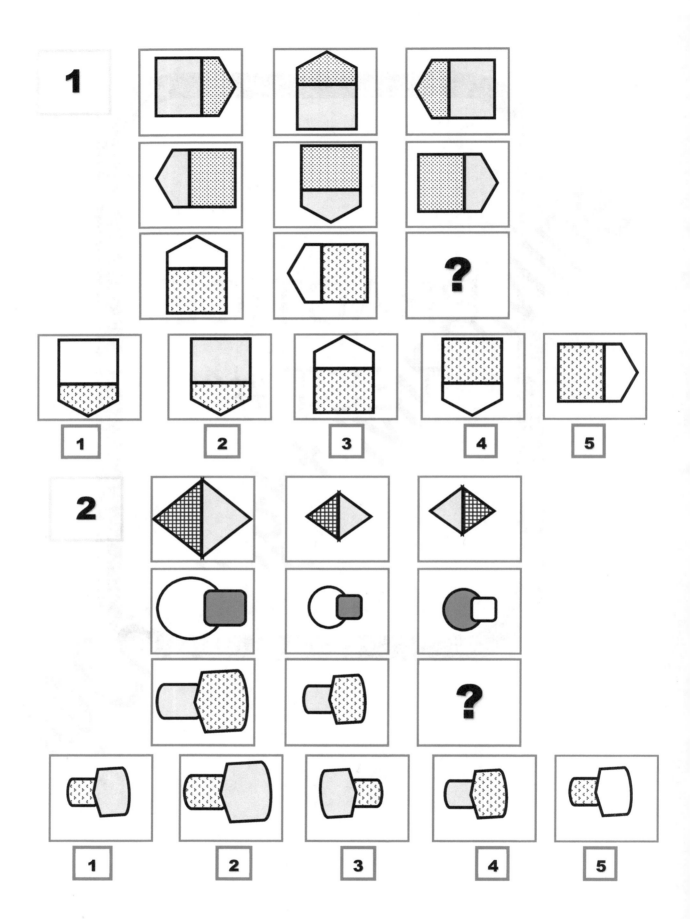

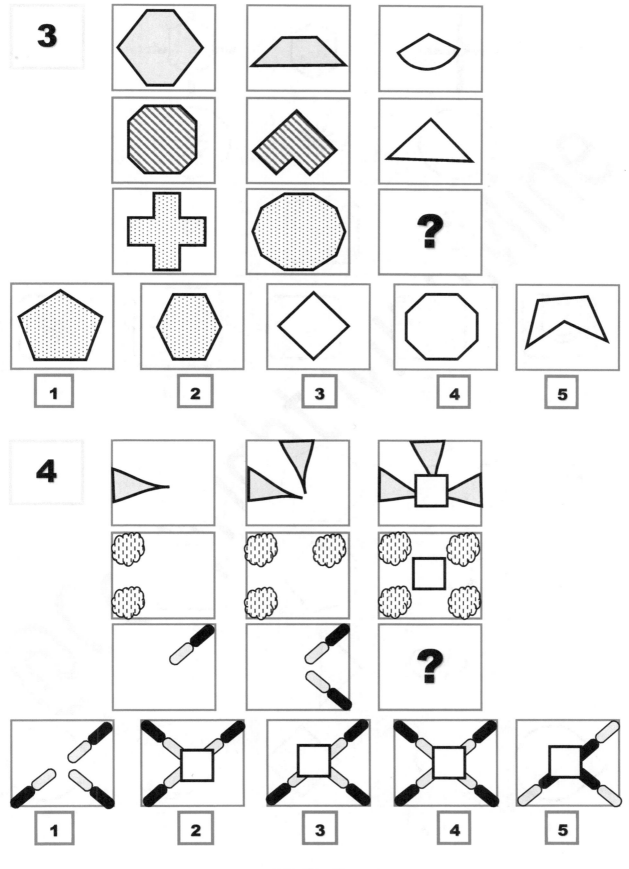

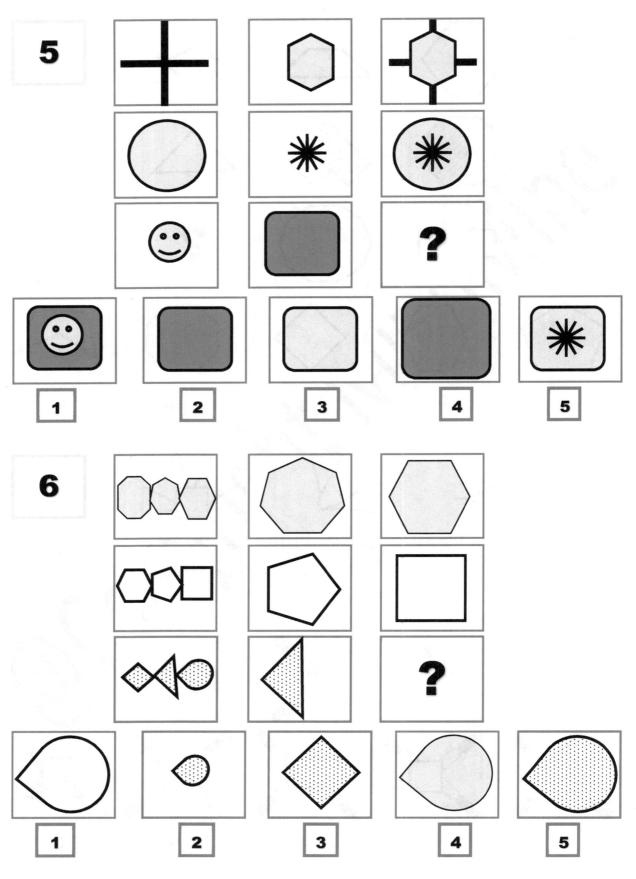

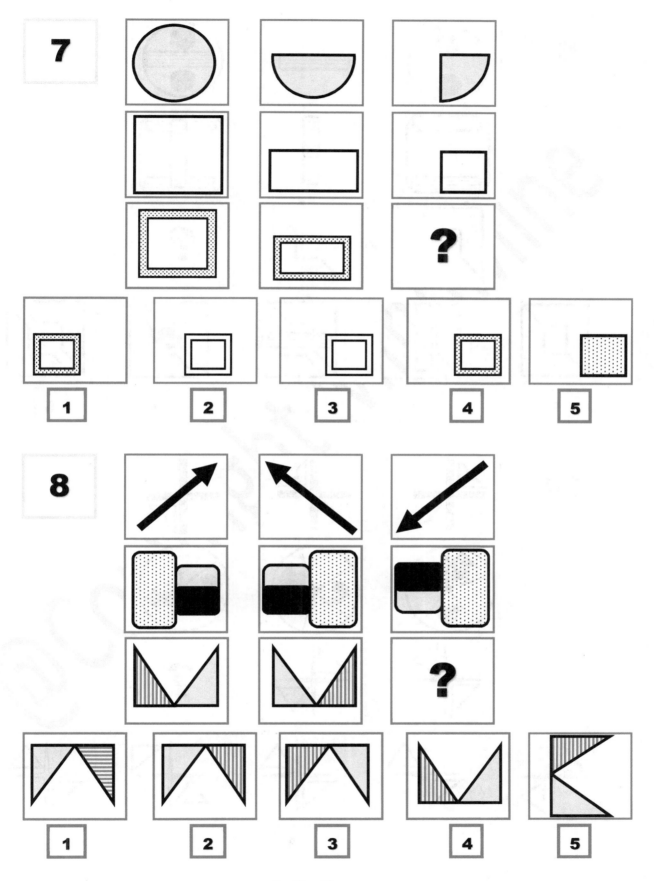

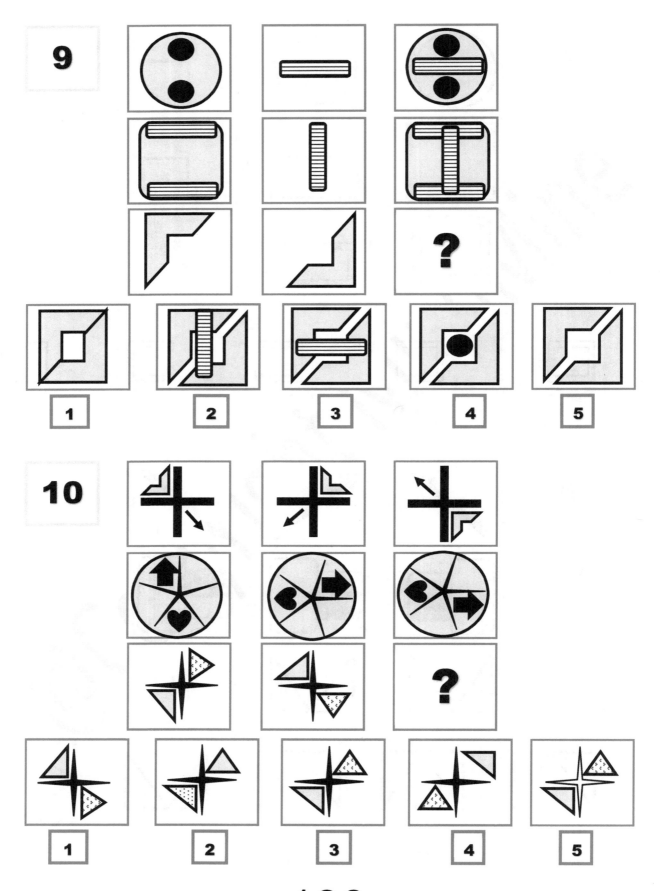

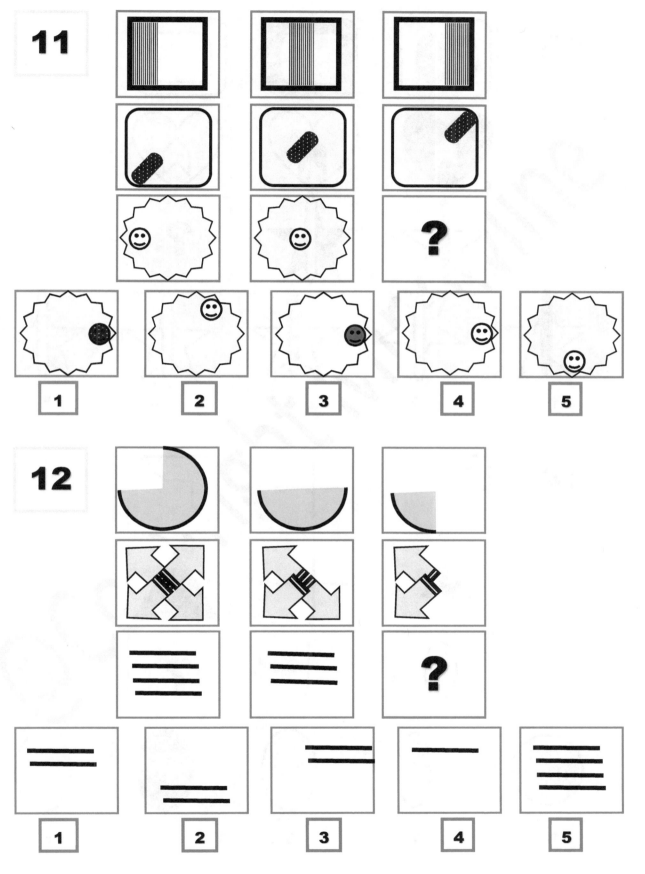

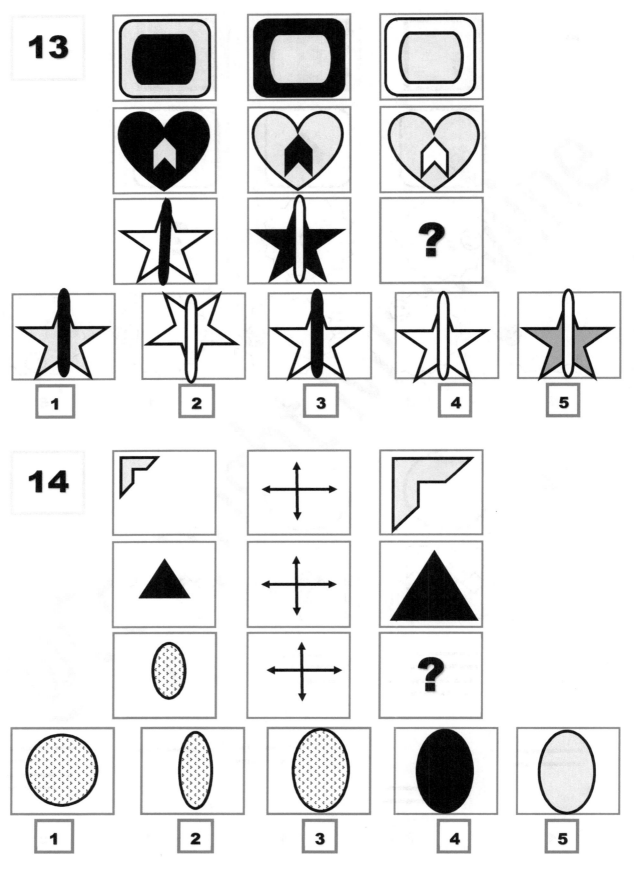

15

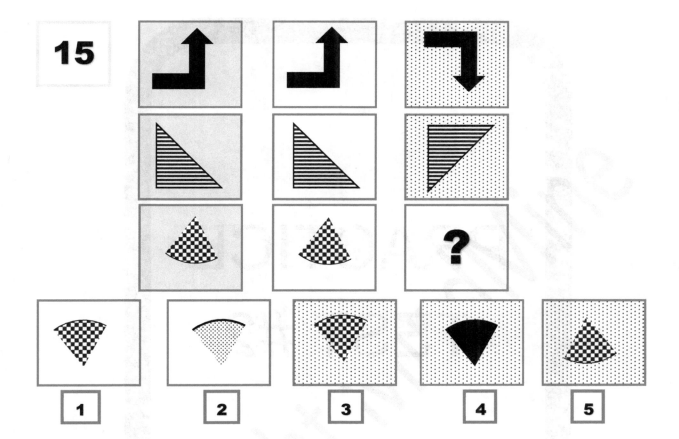

PRACTICE
TEST #2

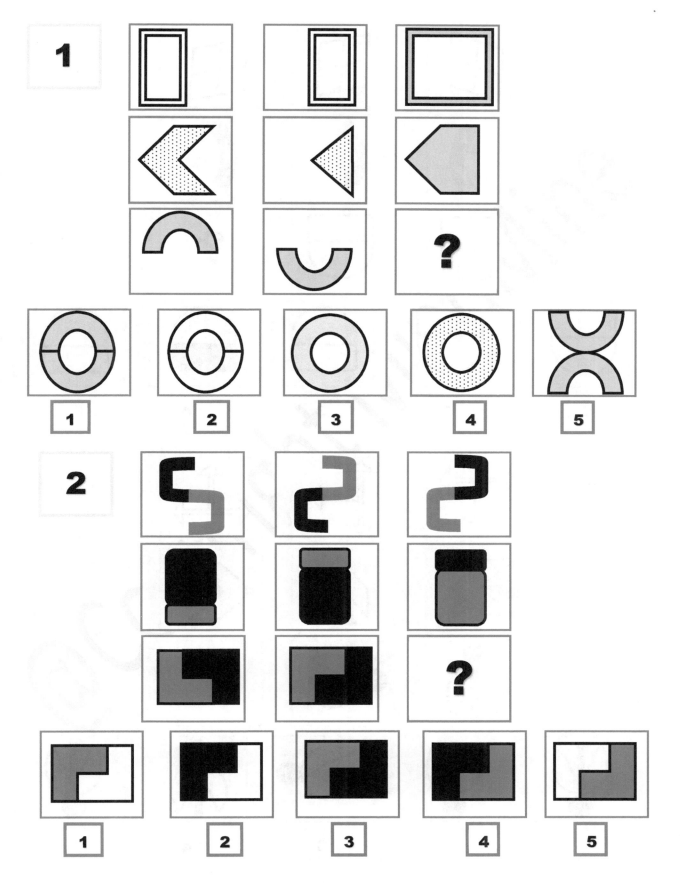

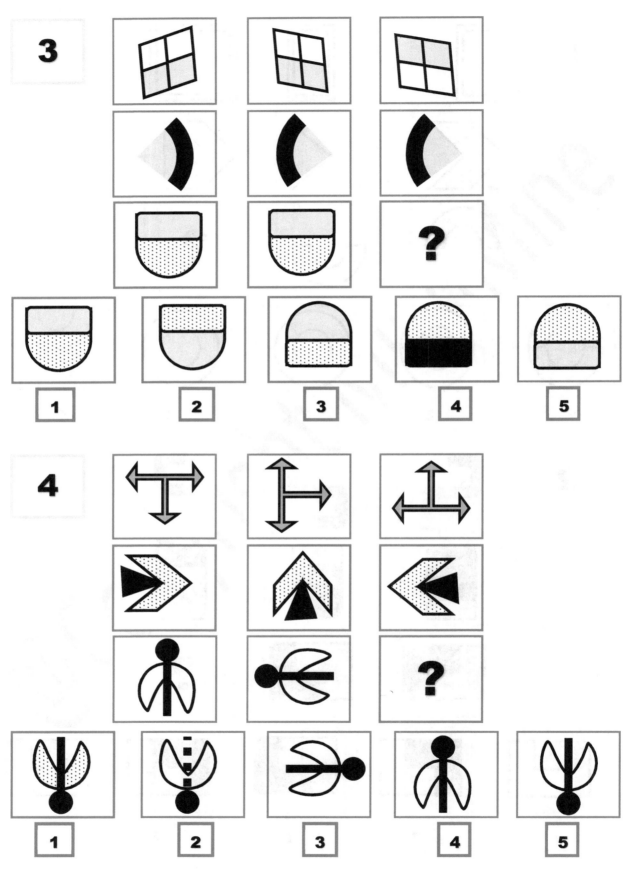

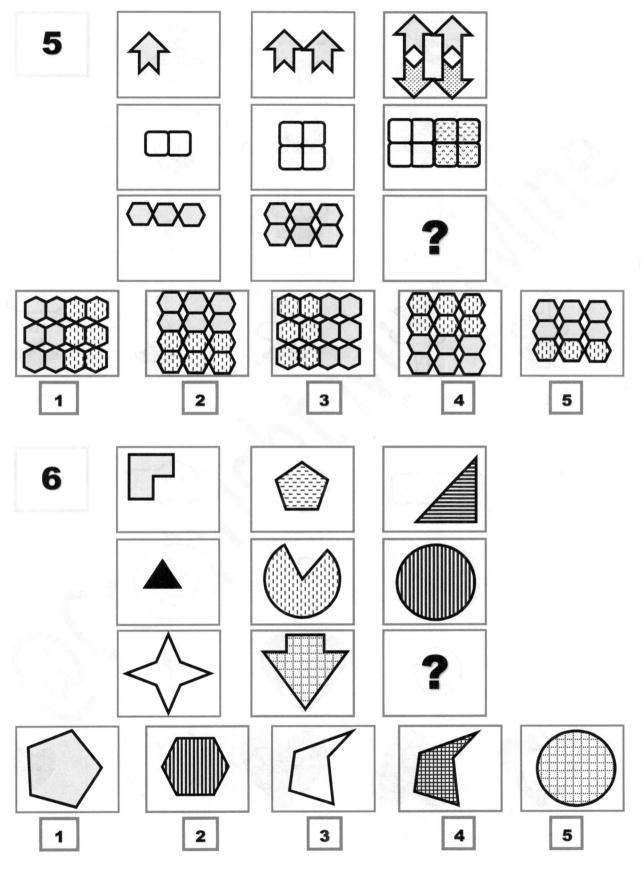

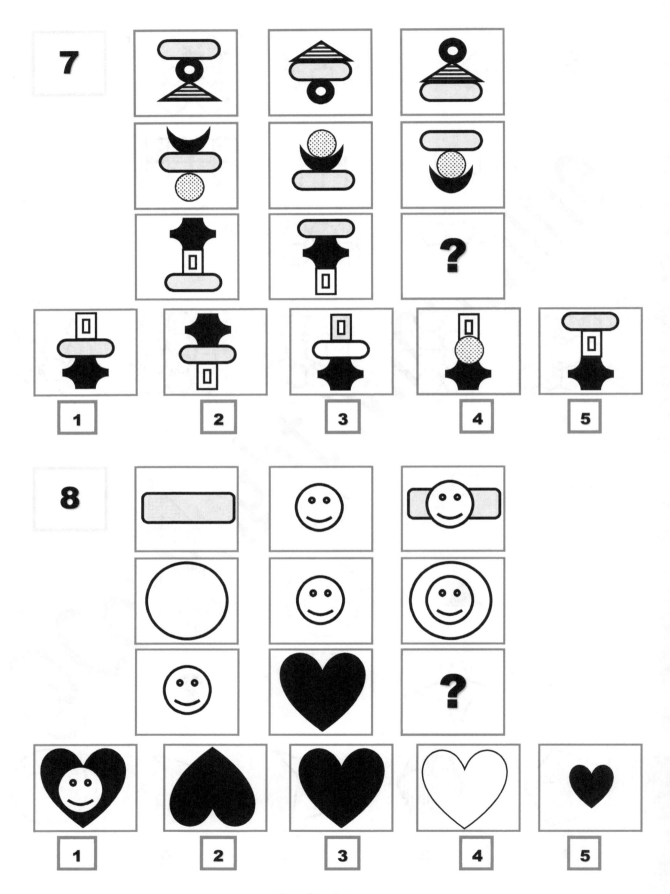

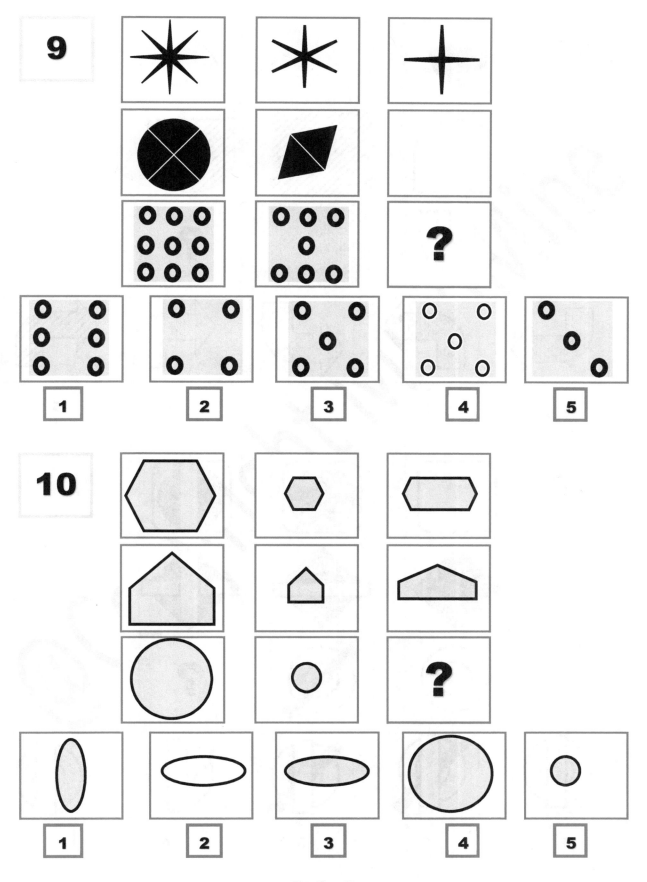

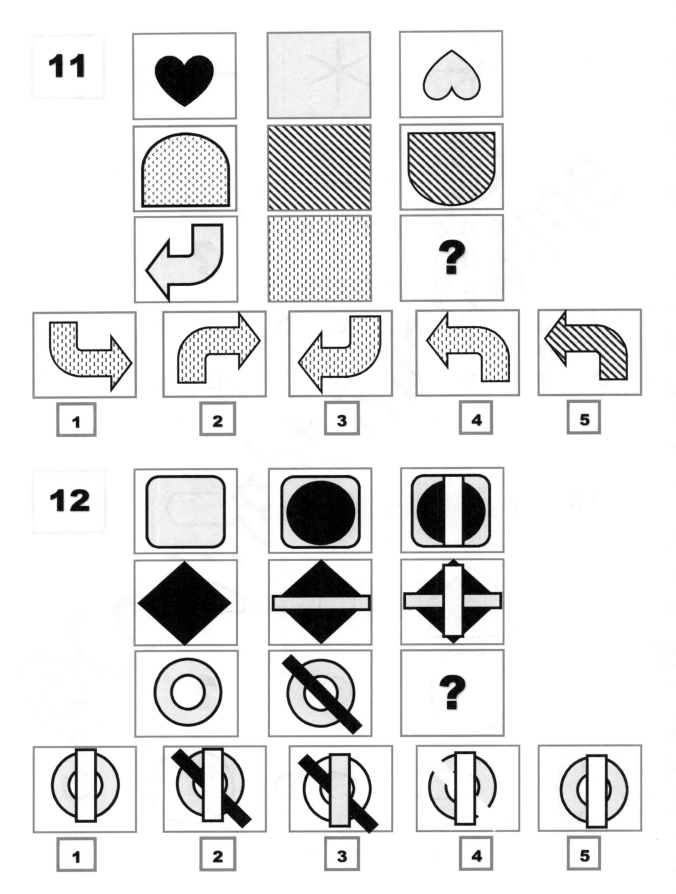

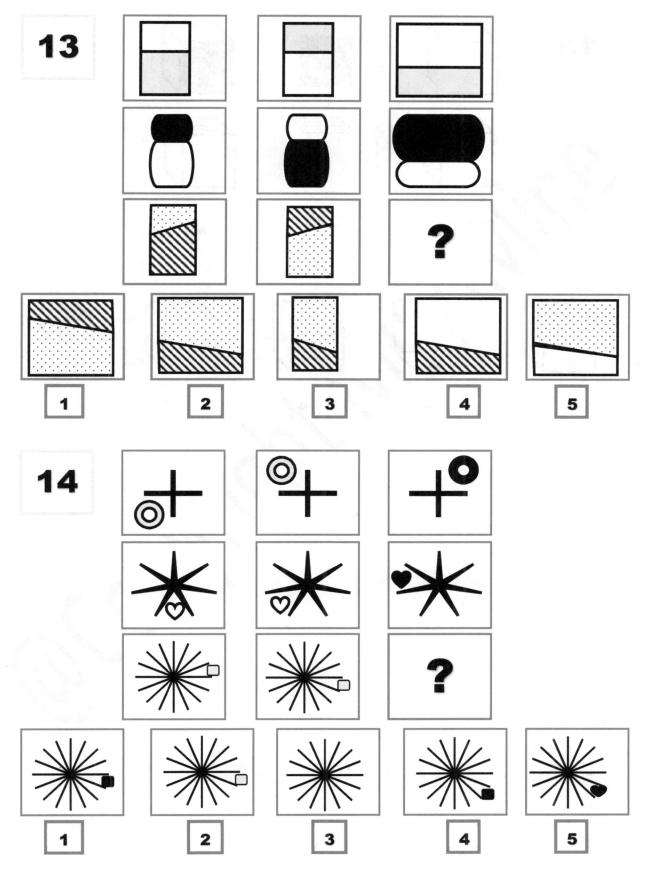

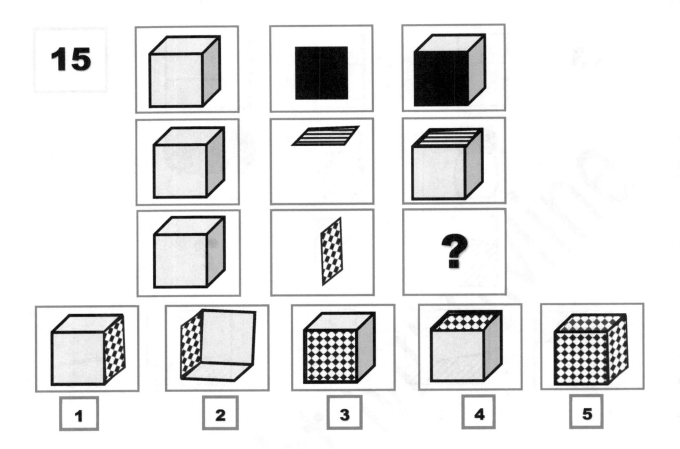

ANSWERS

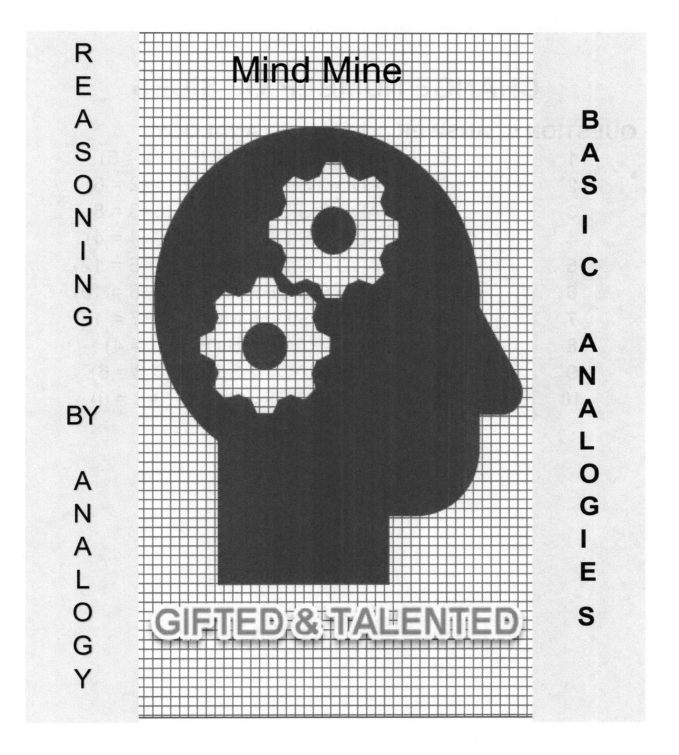

Mind Mine

REASONING

BY

ANALOGY

BASIC ANALOGIES

GIFTED & TALENTED

CHANGE NUMBER OF SIDES

QUESTION #	ANSWER	ANALOGY
1	D	ADD 1 SIDE MORE (4+1 = 5)
2	C	ADD 2 SIDES MORE (4+2 = 6)
3	D	ADD 3 SIDES MORE (5+3 = 8)
4	B	ADD 4 SIDES MORE (0+4 = 4)
5	A	ADD 5 SIDES MORE (7+5 = 12)
6	C	ADD 6 SIDES MORE (4+6 = 10)
7	A	ADD 7 SIDES MORE (5+7 = 12)
8	C	SUBTRACT 1 SIDE (5-1 = 4)
9	A	SUBTRACT 2 SIDES (8-2 = 6)
10	D	SUBTRACT 2 SIDES (3-3 = 0)

CHANGE COLOR

QUESTION #	ANSWER	ANALOGY
1	D	CHANGE COLOR(FILL) TO WHITE
2	A	CHANGE COLOR(FILL) TO GRAY ** Solve Left to Right**
3	B	CHANGE COLOR(PATTERN) TO HORIZONTAL LINES
4	C	CHANGE COLOR(PATTERN) TO DIAGONAL LINES ** A – is not the correct pattern **
5	B	CHANGE COLOR(OUTLINE) TO DOTTED LINES
6	A	CHANGE COLOR(OUTLINE) TO SOLID LINE
7	C	CHANGE COLOR(FILL) TO WHITE ** Solve Left to Right**
8	A	CHANGE COLOR(FILL) TO WHITE ** Solve Left to Right**
9	C	CHANGE COLOR(FILL) TO GRAY ** Solve Left to Right**
10	D	CHANGE COLOR(PATTERN) TO DOTS

216

CHANGE SIZE

QUESTION #	ANSWER	ANALOGY
1	B	MAKE BIG (Stretch Width & Height)
2	C	MAKE BIG (Stretch Width & Height)
3	A	MAKE BIG (Stretch Width & Height)
4	A	MAKE BIG (Stretch Width & Height)
5	C	MAKE BIG (Stretch Width & Height)
6	B	MAKE SMALL (Squeeze Width & Height)
7	A	MAKE SMALL (Squeeze Width & Height)
8	D	MAKE SMALL
9	B	MAKE SMALL (Squeeze Width & Height)
10	C	MAKE SMALL

FLIP (REFLECTION)

QUESTION #	ANSWER	ANALOGY
1	C	FLIP UPSIDE DOWN
2	D	FLIP UPSIDE DOWN
3	B	FLIP UPSIDE DOWN
4	B	FLIP UPSIDE DOWN
5	C	FLIP UPSIDE DOWN
6	A	FLIP UPSIDE DOWN
7	C	FLIP UPSIDE DOWN
8	D	FLIP UPSIDE DOWN
9	B	FLIP UPSIDE DOWN
10	C	FLIP UPSIDE DOWN ** if "C" is not given, "A" becomes right answer. Analogy: Generic FLIP

CUT

QUESTION #	ANSWER	ANALOGY
1	B	CUT BOTTOM
2	C	CUT TOP
3	D	CUT RIGHT
4	B	CUT LEFT
5	C	CUT BOTTOM
6	D	CUT TOP
7	C	CUT TOP DIAGONALLY
8	A	CUT RIGHT
9	B	CUT BOTTOM
10	B	CUT TOP

ADD/REMOVE

QUESTION #	ANSWER	ANALOGY
1	C	ADD A WHITE TRAINGLE INSIDE
2	A	ADD A WHITE CYLINDER INSIDE
3	D	ADD A WHITE SMILEY AT BOTTOM-MIDDLE
4	A	ADD A WHITE OCTAGON IN THE MIDDLE
5	B	ADD A DOTTED, POINTING UP TRAINAGLE INSIDE
6	A	ADD A BLACK VERTICAL STRIP
7	D	ADD A BLCK BOX OUTSIDE
8	A	ADD A SMALLER SAME SHAPE WITH WHITE COLOR INSIDE
9	A	ADD A SMALLER SAME SHAPE WITH WHITE COLOR INSIDE
10	C	ADD A SMALLER SAME SHAPE (DONUT) WITH WHITE COLOR INSIDE

MOVE

QUESTION #	ANSWER	ANALOGY
1	C	MOVE RIGHT ALL THE WAY
2	A	MOVE DOWN ALL THE WAY
3	B	MOVE UP ALL THE WAY
4	D	MOVE LEFT ALL THE WAY
5	C	MOVE RIGHT HALF THE WAY
6	C	MOVE LEFT HALF THE WAY
7	B	MOVE UP HALF THE WAY
8	B	MOVE DOWN HALF THE WAY
9	D	MOVE DOWN HALF THE WAY
10	C	MOVE UP ALL THE WAY

SWAP

QUESTION #	ANSWER	ANALOGY
1	B	SEND BACK (SWAP POSITION)
2	A	SWAP COLOR
3	C	SWAP PLACE
4	B	SWAP COLOR
5	A	SWAP COLOR
6	D	SWAP COLOR ** Note: Analogy could be Flip sideways. But "B" is not Flipped
7	A	SWAP COLOR
8	D	SWAP COLOR
9	C	SEND BACK (SWAP POSITION)
10	A	SEND BACK (SWAP POSITION)

TURN

QUESTION #	ANSWER	ANALOGY
1	C	TURN CLOCKWISE
2	A	TURN COUNTER CLOCKWISE
3	B	TURN CLOCKWISE
4	C	TURN COUNTER CLOCKWISE
5	D	TURN CLOCKWISE
6	B	TURN COUNTER CLOCKWISE
7	B	TURN CLOCKWISE
8	A	TURN CLOCKWISE
9	B	TURN CLOCKWISE Note: Example Analogy work for both clockwise and counter clockwise.
10	C	TURN COUNTER CLOCKWISE

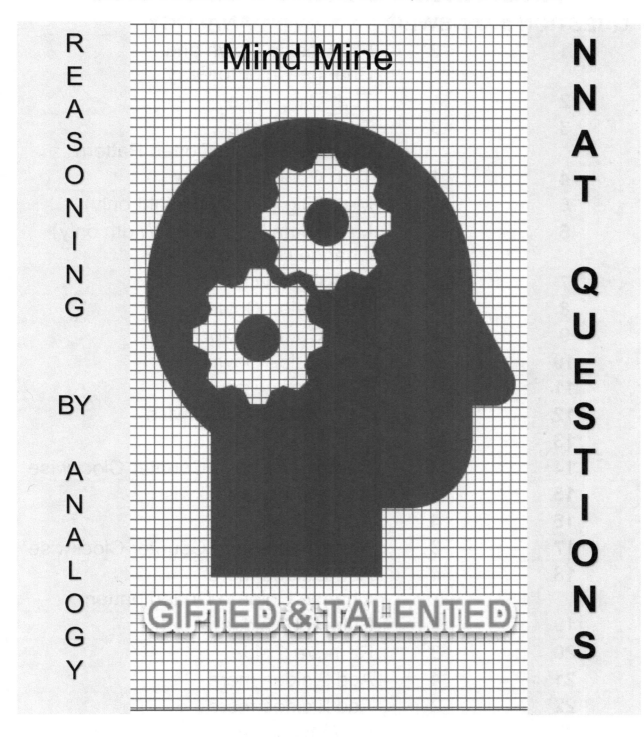

Mind Mine

REASONING BY ANALOGY

NNAT QUESTIONS

GIFTED & TALENTED

ANSWERS TO NNAT QUESTIONS

QUESTION #	ANSWER	ANALOGY
1	2	Flip Upside Down and Change Color to Gray
2	4	Turn Clockwise
3	5	Turn Clockwise Change Color to Dotted Pattern
4	1	Turn Counter Clockwise
5	2	Make Big (Stretch Height only)
6	5	Make Small (Squeeze Width only) Change Color to WHITE
7	3	Turn Clockwise
8	2	Flip Upside Down
9	4	Turn Counter Clockwise
10	5	Flip Upside Down
11	1	Turn Clockwise
12	3	Turn Counter Clockwise
13	2	Turn Clockwise
14	3	Remove a shape Counter Clockwise
15	5	Add a shape Clockwise
16	4	Add a shape
17	3	Remove a shape Counter Clockwise
18	4	Add 2 sides more Change Color to Dotted pattern
19	3	Subtract 2 sides
20	3	Remove 1 side
21	4	Add 2 sides more
22	2	Add 2 sides more
23	2	Move black vertical strip Half the way to LEFT

225

ANSWERS TO NNAT QUESTIONS

QUESTION #	ANSWER	ANALOGY
24	5	Move white circle Half the way to DOWN
25	4	Turn Clockwise
26	3	Move white strip half the way to DOWN
27	5	Move circles half the way to LEFT
28	3	Swap Color
29	4	Change Black Color to Dotted pattern
30	3	Swap Color
31	5	Swap Color
32	2	Swap Color
33	4	Swap Color
34	2	Swap Color
35	1	Cut the right half
36	3	Cut the left half
37	5	Cut the bottom half
38	2	Add the bottom half
39	1	Add the top half
40	3	Flip figure in 1st box Upside down
41	2	Change color to dotted pattern
42	5	Turn Clockwise Change color to dotted pattern
43	4	Flip Upside down Change Color/Pattern to Diagonal lines
44	5	Flip Upside down
45	3	Flip Upside down
46	1	Turn Counter Clockwise

ANSWERS TO NNAT QUESTIONS

QUESTION #	ANSWER	ANALOGY
47	2	Flip Sideways
48	5	Flip Sideways
49	4	Flip Upside down
50	3	Swap Color
51	5	Swap Position (Send Back)
52	5	Swap Position (Send Back)
53	3	Swap Place
54	3	Swap Color
55	5	Swap Place
56	1	Swap Color
57	2	Flip Upside down
58	2	Flip Upside down
59	2	Swap Color
60	1	Send Back
61	5	Bring Front
62	3	Bring Front
63	4	Move top figure to bottom
64	1	Move top figure to bottom
65	3	Move bottom figure to top
66	1	Move left most black rectangle all the way to the right
67	2	Move left most figure all the way to the right
68	4	Add a row below with 5 figures (one more figure than previous row, 4+1 = 5)
69	4	Remove top row

227

ANSWERS TO NNAT QUESTIONS

QUESTION #	ANSWER	ANALOGY
70	5	Add a row above with 3 figures (one more figure than previous row, 2+1 = 3)
71	4	Remove the bottom row
72	2	Add one more figure (4+1 = 5)
73	5	Remove one figure
74	2	Remove one figure from top
75	3	Add one figure
76	3	Stretch sideways
77	5	Stretch vertically
78	2	Stretch vertically and sideways (Make Big)
79	4	Stretch diagonally
80	2	Stretch horizontally (only horizontal rectangle, not the vertical rectangle)
81	5	Place 1st figure over 2nd figure
82	3	Place 2nd figure over 1st figure
83	1	Separate 1st figure into two individual figures
84	5	Place 2nd figure over 1st figure
85	5	Place 2nd figure over 1st figure
86	2	Separate 1st figure into two individual figures
87	2	Place 1st figure over 2nd figure
88	5	Place 1st figure over 2nd figure
89	4	Place 2nd figure over 1st figure
90	3	Join 1st and 2nd figures
91	1	Flip 2nd figure upside down and place over 1st figure

ANSWERS TO NNAT QUESTIONS

QUESTION #	ANSWER	ANALOGY
92	4	Flip 1st figure upside down and place over 2nd figure
93	1	Make 2nd figure small, Flip upside down and place over 1st figure
94	3	Make 1st figure big, make 2nd figure small, Place 2nd figure over 1st figure
95	5	Make 1st figure big, make 2nd figure small, Place 2nd figure over 1st figure Answer Choice 2 is incorrect. Star is flipped upside down which is wrong.
96	4	Place 2nd figure over 1st figure
97	1	Place 2nd figure over 1st figure
98	5	Place 2nd figure over 1st figure
99	1	Place 2nd figure over 1st figure
100	3	Place 2nd figure over 1st figure
101	3	Move left most figure all the way to the right
102	2	Move right most figure all the way to the left
103	4	Flip Upside down
104	5	Flip Sideways
105	4	Flip Upside down
106	2	Add 1 side more and change Color to Gray
107	3	Subtract 1 side (7-1 = 6)
108	5	Half the number of sides (Half of 2 is 1)
109	4	Remove a figure (Clockwise)

ANSWERS TO NNAT QUESTIONS

QUESTION #	ANSWER	ANALOGY
110	4	Add another triangle, white color one (Clockwise)
111	5	Remove a figure (Clockwise)
112	2	Add another arrow (Clockwise)
113	2	Remove a figure (Clockwise)
114	3	Add same figure (Counter Clockwise)
115	1	Remove a figure (Clockwise)
116	4	Add same figure (Clockwise)
117	1	Turn Clockwise
118	3	Turn Counter Clockwise
119	5	Move all the way up
120	1	Move half way to the right
121	3	Move half way to the right
122	1	Move half way to the up
123	3	Move all the way to down
124	2	Move half way to the right
125	1	Move all the way to the right
126	4	Move half the way to the down
127	2	Move half the way to the up
128	5	From the 2nd Box take figure with white color, make it big and place it inside first figure
129	4	From the 2nd Box take figure with black color, make it big and place it inside first figure
130	3	Swap Color (inwards to outwards)
131	3	Swap Color of inside 2 figures

ANSWERS TO NNAT QUESTIONS

QUESTION #	ANSWER	ANALOGY
132	5	Change Color/Pattern of first figure with Color/Pattern of 2nd figure
133	1	Change color of 2nd figure with Color of 1st figure
134	5	Change outside figure Color/Pattern in 1st box to match with first figure in 2nd box; Change inside figure Color/Pattern in 1st box to match with 2nd figure in 2nd box;
135	4	Turn 1st figure Clockwise and make it small
136	2	Change Color/Pattern of 2nd figure to match with Color of inside figure in 1st box
137	1	Change Color/Pattern of 2nd figure to match with color of inside figure in 1st box
138	1	Squeeze 1st figure, squeeze 2nd figure; Join two figures together
139	4	Change color/pattern of 1st figure with Color/Pattern of 2nd figure
140	3	Change outline of 1st figure with Color/Pattern of 2nd figure. Answer choice 5 is incorrect. Pay attention to the size
141	5	Add same figure (Clockwise)
142	4	Add same figure (Counter Clockwise)
143	4	Remove a figure (Clockwise)

ANSWERS TO NNAT QUESTIONS

QUESTION #	ANSWER	ANALOGY
144	5	Remove a figure (Counter Clockwise)
145	1	Place 2nd figure over 1st figure
146	5	Place 1st figure over 2nd figure
147	2	The number of sides should match with the number of figures in 1st box. Color/Pattern should match with Color/Pattern of figure in 2nd box.
148	3	Add a row with 1 more figure than previous row, the color/pattern of the figures in the new row should match with the one in the first box.
149	1	Join 1st and 2nd figures together
150	2	Join 1st and 2nd figures together
151	3	Place 2nd figure below the 1st figure
152	4	Flip 1st figure Upside down and place it below the 2nd figure
153	3	Turn Clockwise
154	5	Turn Counter Clockwise
155	1	Triangle with a base of 4 units (1st figure has 3 triangles each with 1 unit of base, 2nd figure has 1 triangle with 1 unit of base; 3+1 = 4 units of total base)
156	5	Turn Clockwise
157	1	Turn Clockwise
158	2	Turn Counter Clockwise
159	5	Move diagonally half the way
160	1	Move half the way to the right
161	3	Turn Clockwise

ANSWERS TO NNAT QUESTIONS		
QUESTION #	**ANSWER**	**ANALOGY**
162	**5**	Place 1st figure over 2nd figure
163	**1**	Flip Upside down
164	**4**	Flip Upside down
165	**5**	Turn Counter Clockwise
166	**2**	Turn Clockwise
167	**3**	Flip Upside down
168	**5**	Flip Upside down
169	**1**	Remove inside figure from 1st box and add gray colored ✖ inside
170	**2**	Change color/pattern of outside figure in 1st box to Dotted pattern and add a white horizontal stripe (▭)
171	**2**	Turn Clockwise
172	**3**	Turn Clockwise
173	**4**	Swap Color
174	**1**	Swap Color
175	**2**	Change Color to dotted pattern
176	**4**	Swap Color
177	**2**	Swap Color
178	**2**	Swap Position (send back)
179	**4**	Remove a figure
180	**5**	Stretch horizontally, only the bottom
181	**3**	Place 1st figure over 2nd figure
182	**3**	Place 2nd figure over 1st figure
183	**2**	Make 1st figure big, 2nd figure small; Place 2nd figure over 1st figure
184	**1**	Place 2nd figure over 1st figure

ANSWERS TO NNAT QUESTIONS

QUESTION #	ANSWER	ANALOGY
		Answer choice 4 is incorrect. Pay attention to position of white figure.
185	5	Take one of the black colored figures from 2nd box, make it big and place it over the 1st figure
186	3	Change color/pattern of outside figure in 1st box to the color of 1st figure in 2nd box; Change color/pattern of inside figure in 1st box to the color/pattern of 2nd figure in 2nd box
187	3	Change the Color/Pattern of the figure in 1st box to the Color/Pattern of the figure in 2nd box
188	2	Move down half the way
189	5	Turn Clockwise
190	2	Remove inside figure from 1st box and add a gray colored ✚
191	2	Stretch Width only
192	5	Squeeze Width only
193	3	Squeeze sideways (diameter) only
194	1	Squeeze height only
195	5	Add another shape Clockwise
196	2	Place 2nd figure over 1st figure

ANSWERS TO NNAT QUESTIONS

QUESTION #	ANSWER	ANALOGY
		Answer choice 1 is incorrect. Pay attention to position of figures in 1st box and 2nd box
197	1	Turn Clockwise
198	5	Turn Counter Clockwise
199	4	Turn Clockwise
200	2	Remove one figure

FULL LENGTH PRACTICE TEST # 1
ANSWERS

QUESTION #	ANSWER	ANALOGY
1	4	Turn Counter Clockwise
2	1	Swap Color
3	5	Half the number of sides (Half of 12 is 6) and Change Color/Pattern to White
4	3	Add another shape Clockwise and add a white square in the middle
5	2	Place 2nd figure over 1st figure
6	5	Subtract one side (3-1=2 sides)
7	4	Cut and remove left half of the figure
8	2	Flip Upside down
9	5	Put 2nd figure over 1st figure
10	3	Flip Upside down
11	4	Move half the way to the right
12	1	Remove 1 figure (line)
13	4	Change Black color shape to White color
14	3	Make Big
15	3	Change background Color/Pattern to dotted pattern and Flip Upside down

FULL LENGTH PRACTICE TEST # 2
ANSWERS

QUESTION #	ANSWER	ANALOGY
1	3	Join 1st and 2nd figures, Remove the adjoining line, Change Color to Gray
2	4	Swap Color
3	5	Flip Upside down
4	5	Turn Counter Clockwise
5	2	Add same number of shapes on the side or below with a dotted pattern
6	4	Subtract 2 sides (7-2= 5-sided shape), use the same Pattern as that of figure in 2nd box with a black color
7	1	Move the bottom most figure to top
8	3	Place the 2nd figure over 1st figure
9	3	Remove 2 sides or parts (7-2 = 5)
10	3	Stretch sideways (diameter)
11	4	Flip the 1st figure, Change the Color/Pattern to match with 2nd figure
12	2	Add a white vertical strip in front of figure in 2nd box

QUESTION #	ANSWER	ANALOGY
13	2	Flip Upside down and stretch Width only
14	4	Turn Clockwise, change Color to black
15	1	Join 1st and 2nd figures

Other ways to use this book

15 Mini Practice Tests

Questions are organized by each individual concept. Picking 15 questions randomly and solving them out of order serve as a mini practice test. **About 12 mini practice tests** can be generated.

500 Additional Questions

- After solving each question, Write down the answer in the box with **"?"**.

- Now cover first box on first row and solve question. This will generate 200 additional questions.

- Now cover 2nd box on first row and solve question. This will generate 200 additional questions.

- Now cover First box on 2nd row and solve question. This will generate 200 additional questions.

- Now cover 2nd box on 2nd row and solve question. This will generate 200 additional questions.

Note: Additional questions Do Not have answer choices.

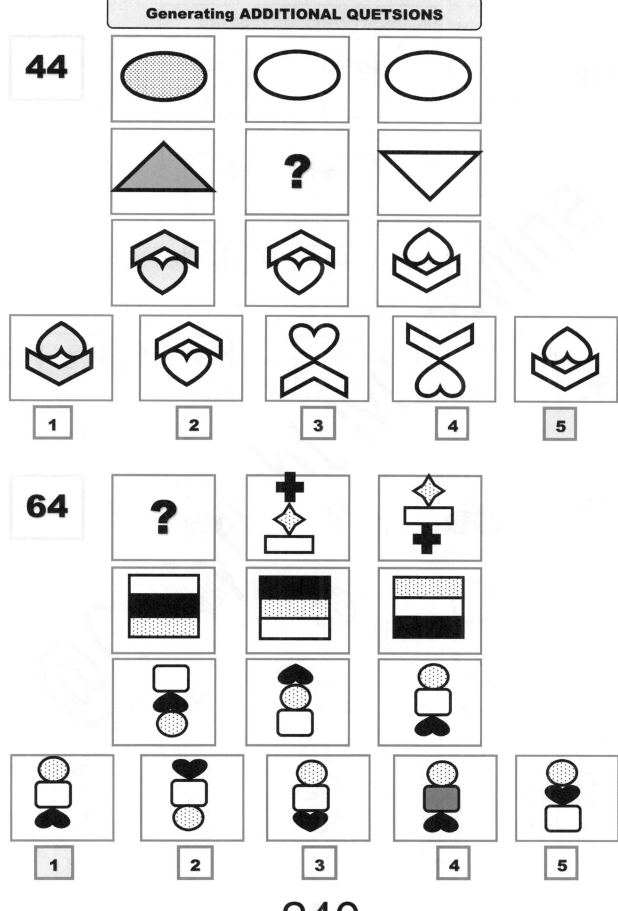

240

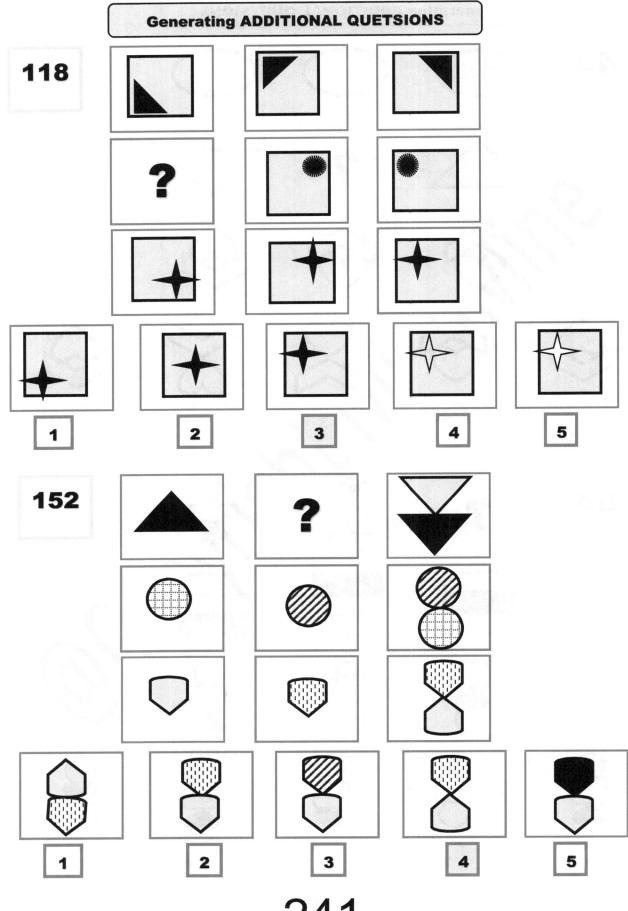

Additional Help

Have a question? You can reach author directly at
mindmineauthor@gmail.com

Made in United States
Troutdale, OR
06/12/2024

20526317R00139